KAREN L. MAPP, ANNE T. HENDERSON,
MARTHA C. FRANCO, AND SUZA

MW01070589

EVERYONE WINS!

The Evidence for
Family-School Partnerships
& Implications for Practice

■ SCHOLASTIC

We dedicate this book to our dear friend and late colleague, Don Davies, the Founding Father of our field of family engagement. Don's farsighted vision went far beyond the parent-child-teacher relationship to encompass the entire community, state, and federal context. His kind, wise, and firm demeanor made him a marvelous mentor to hundreds who were guided by his keen understanding, and an inspiration to thousands more. We stand on his shoulders and continue his legacy by fighting for an education system that is responsive to, and equitable for all children, families, and communities.

Founder, Institute for Responsive Education (IRE)
and the League of Schools Reaching Out (1973–2007)

Co-Director, Center on Families, Communities, Schools,
and Children's Learning (1990–1996)

Co-Founder, International Network of Scholars on School,
Family, and Community Partnerships (INET) (1991)

Senior Vice President and Publisher: Tara Welty
Editorial Director: Sarah Longhi
Development Editor: Raymond Coutu
Senior Editor: Shelley Griffin
Production Editor: Danny Miller
Creative Director: Tannaz Fassihi
Interior Designer: Maria Lilja
Editorial Assistant: Samantha Unger

Cover illustration by Guillaume Gennet.

Photos ©: 12: sturti/Getty Images; 17: JGI/Jamie Grill/Getty Images; 22: vm/Getty Images; 24: courtesy of Anne Henderson; 25: Courtesy of Human Capital Research Collaborative/cpcp3.org; 36: Maskot/Getty Images; 41: Courtesy of Washington State Association of Head Start and ECEAP; 43: SolStock/Getty Images; 53: Courtney Hale/Getty Images; 65: IPGGutenbergUKLtd/Getty Images; 80: courtesy of Anne Henderson; 81: SolStock/Getty Images; 99: Maskot/Getty Images; 103: mixetto/Getty Images; 107: SDI Productions/Getty Images; 109: FatCamera/Getty Images; 112: Courtesy of the Parent-Teacher Home Visit Project. All other photos © Shutterstock.

Additional credits ©: pages 44, 89: Excerpt and graphic adapted from *A Match on Dry Grass* copyright © 2011 by Mark R. Warren and Karen L. Mapp. Used by permission of Oxford University Press, Inc.; 48: Graphic adapted from Kidsburgh.org. Used by permission; 66-67: Excerpt adapted from Parent Teacher Home Visits, pthvp.org. Used by permission; 82-83: Excerpt adapted from *The Way We Do School: The Making of Oakland's Full-Service Community School District* by M. McLaughlin, K. Fehrer, and J. Leos-Urbel copyright © 2020 by the President and Fellows of Harvard College. Used by permission of Harvard Education Press; 91: Graphic adapted from "Data Inquiry for Equitable Collaboration: The Case of Neighborhood House's Data Carousel" copyright © 2015 by University of Washington. Used by permission; 93: Excerpt adapted from *Just Schools: Building Equitable Collaborations With Families and Communities* by Ann M. Ishimaru copyright © 2020 by Teachers College, Columbia University. Used by permission of Teachers College Press.
All rights reserved.

Scholastic Inc., 557 Broadway, New York, NY 10012

CONTENTS

ACKNOWLEDGMENTS

Because this book is the fifth in the *Evidence* series, it has a long history, giving us many wonderful people to recognize and thank. It began with the National Committee for Citizens in Education (NCCE) in 1981. A citizen advocacy group, NCCE championed parent and community voice in education policy. At the time there was little research on whether this was a good idea. There was research, however, on the benefits of involving families in their children's learning. The first three editions (1981, 1987, and 1994) bolstered NCCE's contention that hearing from families was critical to good policy and practice. Each one had *Evidence* in the title. Many thanks to Carl Marburger, Stanley Salett, and Bill Rioux for their insistent support and guidance.

The fourth edition came about when Karen, then the President of the Institute for Responsive Education, called Anne, the author of the first three, to nudge her that "the *Evidence* is getting out of date." Anne responded that she would do a new one only if Karen would be her partner. Karen persuaded the Southwest Educational Development Laboratory to fund and publish *A New Wave of Evidence,* which came out in 2002. Many thanks to Catherine Jordan, Lacy Wood and the SEDL staff for shepherding that project.

After that, Anne and Karen collaborated on several projects, including *Beyond the Bake Sale: The Essential Guide to Family-School Partnerships*, our book on how to put the evidence into practice. (Henderson, Mapp, Johnson, and Davies, 2007) Finally, we realized that the *Evidence* was getting *really* out of date, and we approached Scholastic about publishing this fifth edition. Karen recruited our three co-authors, Stephany Cuevas, Suzanna Ewert and Martha C. Franco, from among her students at Harvard, and directed our efforts.

All five authors would like to thank the team at Scholastic for their unwavering support during this project. Special thanks to Ray Coutu, Sarah Longhi, Shelley Griffin, Danny Miller, Tannaz Fassihi, Maria Lilja, and Karen Baicker for their excellent editing, guidance, creative design, and stewardship.

We also want to thank colleagues who responded to our reader survey, sent us copies of their studies, recommended other studies, and otherwise encouraged and supported our work: Gillian Baxter, Eyal Bergman, Rosa Briceno, Michele Brooks, Judy Carson, Ilene Carver, Maggie Caspe, Norm Fruchter, Joanna Geller, Brooke Gill, Janet Goodall, Soo Hong, Kathy Hoover Dempsey, Darcy Hutchins, Ann Ishimaru, Betsy Leborious, Veronica Merion, Ron Mirr, Danielle Perry, Wendy Perez, Helen Westmoreland, Sherri Wilson, and many more.

Karen: I would like to thank my partner, Donal Fox, for being there at all times, especially when I've stumbled, to provide that steady hand, warm embrace, words of encouragement and outpouring of love when I need it most. I'd also like to thank my writing partners, Anne, Stephany, Suzanna, and "Marta:" I learn as much from you as I hope you learn from me. Thank you for your patience and putting up with me and my crazy schedule!

Anne: I would like to thank three generations: My parents, Evie and Frank Thompson, who showed me what it means to have a close and loving family. My husband, Basil Henderson, who has five times endured overflowing piles of books, reports, monographs, and drafts, with grace and humor. The first edition he dubbed "The Evidence Glows" (on my computer monitor); the third was "The Evidence is Out of Control," and this one is "The Evidence Speaks for Itself." My daughter, Amy-Louise, her husband Len Parker, and my two grandchildren, Thompson and Aleta, now in public school, who have taken me back to the beginning all over again.

Martha: I would like to thank my mother, Ana G, Candido, sister, Estefany N. Franco, and the educators, youth, and communities that have shaped me.

Stephany: Thank you to my family—my parents Carmen Cuevas and Rafael Figueroa, sisters Athina Cuevas and Daisy Figueroa, and *tía* aunt Cukis Figueroa—for always modeling the importance of familial support. Thank you, Alex Torres, for keeping me grounded. And thank you to my friends, colleagues, and the educators in my life for sharing the importance of family engagement work.

Suzanna: Huge thanks to my family, Rex and Cathy Ewert, and Carl Ewert and Kate Dopkin, for supporting, encouraging, and being there for me throughout the work on my first publication. Also, thanks to Alex and Thomas for sound-boarding and commiseration through pandemic park beers and phone calls.

Anne, Stephany, and Suzanna want to thank Karen for her leadership, and all four of us want to thank our fellow team members for persevering patiently through innumerable Zoom meetings, Google Docs, and emailed drafts. Working with each other remotely has been a rewarding challenge. Here's to the day that we can all meet in person!

—**Karen Mapp, Anne Henderson, Stephany Cuevas,
Martha C. Franco, and Suzanna Ewert**
June 2022

FOREWORD
by VITO J. BORRELLO

Welcome to *Everyone Wins!* It is a privilege to write the foreword for a book that so compellingly addresses the challenges, barriers, progress, and opportunities in advancing family and community engagement in education. By reading this seminal publication, I'm confident you will become an even stronger advocate for policies and practices that embrace the role of families in achieving high-quality education for all students.

Commonsense but not common practice. Perhaps that phrase best describes the historic lack of prioritization of family engagement strategies in education. Consider these questions:

- Is it reasonable to conclude that no adult understands their child better than a parent or caregiver?

- Is it reasonable to conclude that *all* families have knowledge and insight about their children, no matter their race, culture, socioeconomic status, or education level?

- If so, then, as a society, shouldn't we be preparing educators to leverage that knowledge and insight to improve learning?

What seems so commonsensical has historically been a missed opportunity. Schools have too often focused family engagement efforts on public relations and "fixing families" rather than engaging families as partners. Rarely, in my experience, do educational systems treat families as experts who bring unique assets to the table. Further, for some families, particularly low-income families with limited educational experiences as well as families that have been underserved and marginalized, systems have often disregarded them entirely. When the COVID-19 pandemic challenged the world, children were forced to learn in their homes, and the critical role of families to ensure their success was brought to light like never before.

Research conducted by the organization that I lead, the National Association for Family, School, and Community Engagement (NAFSCE), in partnership with the FrameWorks Institute, indicates that many people believe that family engagement depends on how much the adults in a child's life—especially parents and teachers—"care." While caring is essential, it is not enough. Educators must know *how* to engage families and have the resources they need, including adequate time and supportive leadership. What's more, as this book so effectively demonstrates, this work benefits families, teachers, students, and schools. For *everyone to win*, we must be strategic and intentional in building the capacity of educators, school leaders, and communities, as well as families themselves, to engage families as educational partners. Think of it as a spacecraft launch. Just as engineers, mathematicians, and physicists must work together to send astronauts into the stratosphere, families, schools, and communities must work together for children to take off.

Thanks to the tireless work and leadership of many people, there has been—and continues to be—tremendous progress in family engagement as a way to support learning. The lead authors of this book, Karen Mapp and Anne Henderson, are icons in the field, authoring the bestselling book *Beyond the Bake Sale: The Essential Guide to Family-School Partnerships*, a game changer in transforming our understandings about family engagement. Both authors are founding board members of NAFSCE, and Anne is currently vice chair. Karen developed the highly regarded Dual Capacity-Building Framework and founded the Harvard Family Engagement Institute, which has been attended by thousands of educational leaders, researchers, policy makers, and practitioners, including me.

As NAFSCE's executive director, and through my leadership roles over the past 27 years, I can attest to the progress in family engagement and the realization from the broader education field about the need for improved family engagement policy and practice. Innovations in family engagement are occurring at all levels of education, including the U.S. Department of Education and other federal agencies, state agencies, institutes for higher education, teachers' unions, school districts and schools, and Head Starts, as well as community-based and parent-leadership organizations.

Everyone Wins! is a testament to the progress we've made and the opportunities that lie before us to transform and elevate American education. The research is clear: When we implement effective family engagement practices, everyone wins. Families benefit. Teachers and principals benefit. Entire school communities benefit. Most important, our children benefit.

Everyone Wins! provides a landscape analysis of compelling research, highlights best practices, and provides recommendations to make an impact and achieve outcomes. As the authors state, "it's simply not enough to have a strong desire and good intentions." I hope you enjoy this book as much as I did and, in its pages, find inspiration and new ideas. Now is the time to move away from deficit thinking about families and toward equitable partnerships with them that honor their cultures and values and build on assets. Now is the time for education to prioritize family engagement as the essential strategy that research proves it is. Now is the time to embrace *common sense* as the impetus for sustained *common practice*.

—**VITO J. BORRELLO, Executive Director,**
National Association for Family, School,
and Community Engagement (NAFSCE)

EVERYONE WINS! IN SHORT

For 50 years, the evidence has been steadily mounting: Family-school partnerships are essential not only to student success, but also to creating schools that serve all children well.

The studies covered here reveal high-impact practices that have transformational effects on students, educators, families, schools, and communities. When schools intentionally cultivate relationships of trust and respect with families, they create a culture where EVERYONE WINS!

Wins for Students:

- Higher grades and test scores

- Better attendance and engagement in class

- More positive attitudes and behavior

- Greater sense of efficacy and self-esteem

- Higher graduation rates and college/postsecondary attendance

Why? Students feel supported and reassured when the most important adults in their lives are working together to help them learn. When this process starts in early childhood, children's developing confidence and motivation encourage their families to remain involved, setting up a positive cycle that persists from cradle to career.

Wins for Educators:

- Shift from deficit- to asset-based beliefs and mindsets about all students and families

- Increased multicultural awareness and appreciation

- Greater success motivating and engaging students of diverse backgrounds

- More support from families

- Stronger morale and professional satisfaction

Why? Teachers gain insights into their students' strengths and challenges, allowing them to enrich instruction and integrate students' experiences into classroom lessons. Collaborating with families also creates shared purpose and reduces their sense of isolation. School leaders gain valuable skills for communicating and working with families.

Wins for Families:

- Stronger parent-child relationships

- Better rapport with teachers and school staff

- Greater understanding of child's progress and how to help

- More knowledge and skill in advocating for child

- Increased deep and supportive social connections

Why? Families gain skills and confidence in helping their children learn, navigating the school system, generating ideas for improved learning opportunities, and working to change policy and practice. Parents move from seeing themselves as "just a parent" to becoming "role models" and the "go-to people" in their families and community.

Wins for Schools:

- More positive school climate

- Higher morale and greater retention of teachers

- Improved facilities, better curriculum, and higher-quality programs

- More responsive to community concerns

- Better reputation and more support from the community

Why? When schools become more welcoming and inclusive, it transforms school climate in ways that benefit everyone. By engaging families with a spirit of partnership, schools become rooted in and reflecting the lives and experiences of their students, families, and community.

Wins for school districts and communities:

- Reduced suspensions and high-risk behaviors

- Increased family and youth involvement in site-based decisions

- Expanded mental and physical health resources leading to improved health

- High levels of participation in afterschool programs

- Increased high school graduation rate

Why? Listening to students, families, and community members helps school districts and community partners improve their policies and practices because of what they learn. Families are experts on their children, their culture, and their neighborhoods. They know what would make their community a better place to live and raise children.

Putting These Findings Into Practice

Here's what you can do…

1 **Intentionally cultivate relationships of trust and respect.** Center efforts on children's learning and development. Include family partnerships in school-improvement plans that center justice as the long-term goal.

2 **Start family engagement practices when children are young.** Equip families to navigate the system and continue engaging families up to college and career.

3 **Communicate clearly and continuously.** Establish ongoing two-way communication with families, make the information accessible in all languages, and link it to what students are learning.

4 **Focus on equity. Provide extra supports so that all families get what they need to support their children's learning.** Consider the realities of family life, such as childcare, immigration status, and work constraints. Invite families into decision-making as equal partners.

5 **Prepare educators at all levels to work with families of all backgrounds,** both in pre-service and professional development.

6 **Extend networks, partnerships, and opportunities for parent and family leadership.** Collaborate with community organizing efforts to share power with families and leverage outside resources.

INTRODUCTION

We have a vision: a world where family-school-community partnerships are universally practiced as an essential strategy to improve children's learning and to advance equity, so that all children get what they need to succeed.

The time is right. After decades of trying to improve schools through standards-based, test-driven accountability systems, we know that something is missing. New studies, building on a bedrock of earlier research, show that on-the-ground collaboration is more effective than top-down direction. Families are experts on their children, cultures, and neighborhoods. Community organizers offer valuable resources and networks to tap. Teachers and students know what makes their schools better places to work and learn. They all must be at the table!

Meanwhile, momentum is building:

- The federal government is increasing funding for Statewide Family Engagement Centers and 21st Century Community Schools.

- Local and state education agencies are hiring family engagement staff, creating offices to oversee programs and initiatives, and developing policies to foster consistent and effective practice.

- National philanthropies such as the Carnegie Corporation and the W. K. Kellogg Foundation are investing in family engagement programs and innovations.

- Two annual national conferences and a summer institute at Harvard University are convening practitioners, parent leaders, funders, policymakers, community organizations, and public officials to learn about new initiatives and effective practice.

The infrastructure is growing. The Institute for Educational Leadership has developed state and district networks of family engagement leaders as well as the Coalition for Community Schools. The field also has a professional association: the National Association for Family, School, and Community Engagement (NAFSCE). Currently under the direction of Vito J. Borrello, who wrote the foreword for this book, NAFSCE's mission is to advance high-impact policies and practice of family, school, and community engagement. The association is working in several ways to carry out that mission, including teacher preparation and credentialing, parent leadership, social marketing, and Family Math, an initiative to promote family engagement in math teaching and learning.

And research supports that vision. While writing this book, our country endured a devastating pandemic, a traumatic racial reckoning, and highly polarized elections. Building trust and collaboration at the ground level is healing, and the ripple effects benefit the entire community. Family engagement is about far more than caring. It's about actively collaborating as equal partners. When that collaboration is centered on children's academic achievement and healthy social-emotional development, it builds broad consensus. It serves everyone's interest for our children to thrive. So, let's start from there and build on it together.

In this book, we review studies that make a compelling case for investing in evidence-based practices of engaging families—and suggest ways for you to put those practices into action in schools and districts. Building trusting and collaborative relationships with families is key to ensuring students' academic achievement and social-emotional development. And students aren't the only ones who benefit. In schools that are welcoming, respectful, and inclusive of families, teachers, administrators, and the families themselves benefit, too. That is why we called the book *Everyone Wins!*.

Background

In 1966, the sociologist James Coleman dropped a bombshell. His massive study, *Equality of Educational Opportunity*, based on data covering 650,000 students and 3,000 schools, revealed a shocking finding: American public schools were not the pathway to upward mobility they were supposed to be. Instead, they were quite the opposite, reproducing the inequities often found in society. Well-off students tended to rise to the top, while lower-income (especially Black) students tended to stay at the bottom. Family background and socio-economic status (SES) seemed to be the strongest predictors of future success. Although the study's methods and findings have been severely critiqued, its chief contribution has been to raise a critical question: Do our schools make a difference?

This report triggered a torrent of studies that examined how family background and SES influence outcomes. Researchers explored whether interventions to strengthen families and make schools more equitable could improve achievement for low-income children. Although some of those studies focused on "improving" the home environment (or as parents saw it, "fixing" families), many were thoughtful, respectful explorations of what schools could do to work collaboratively with families.

The "Evidence" Series

This book is the fifth installment of the "Evidence" series which has tracked the growth of research on family engagement for decades. *The Evidence Grows: Parent Participation and Student Achievement* (Henderson, 1981), the first in the series, broke new ground by focusing on the positive effects that engaging families have on student learning. Many of the studies it covered were inspired by the landmark Coleman Report.

Some Historical Context

Commissioned by the Civil Rights Act of 1964, the Coleman Report was released when the Civil Rights Movement was in full swing. At the same time, President Lyndon Johnson was waging the War on Poverty. The Elementary and Secondary Education Act (ESEA) of 1965 was inspired by both. Title I, ESEA, "Compensatory Education for Disadvantaged Students," and Head Start and Follow-Through were guided by the War on Poverty watchword, "maximum feasible participation." All three programs required parent advisory councils and other forms of family engagement. The goal was to give low-income communities a voice in improving children's outcomes at school and their prospects in life.

By the late 1970s, reaction to what was seen by some as "burdensome regulation" and "interference with local control" was gaining momentum. After the 1980 presidential election, conservatives had control of both the White House and Congress. War on Poverty programs were dismantled or farmed out to a variety of federal agencies. The ESEA was repealed and replaced with block grants to the states. Ten pages of family-engagement requirements in the Title I program were reduced to a single sentence requiring Title I schools to hold an annual meeting with parents.

Why was parent involvement eliminated? Washington policymakers said parent advisory councils "undermined the authority of local officials" and that, furthermore, there was "no evidence" that involving low-income, poorly educated parents had an impact on student achievement. There *was* evidence, however, in all those studies that followed the Coleman Report and evaluated War on Poverty programs. But no one had yet assembled them into a single persuasive document that could change policy. (For more history about Title I, see: Mapp, Karen L. Title I and Parent Involvement: Lessons from the Past, Recommendations for the Future, Washington DC: Center for American Progress, March 2012.)

Growing Evidence

In 1981, the National Committee for Citizens in Education published *The Evidence Grows*, followed by two more editions, *The Evidence Continues to Grow: Parent Involvement Improves Student Achievement* (Henderson, 1987) and *A New Generation of Evidence: The Family Is Critical to Student Achievement* (Henderson & Berla, 1994). Some key findings included:

- Adding a family engagement component makes early childhood programs, such as Head Start, more effective and their results longer lasting.

- Engaging families strengthens the home learning environment, with positive effects on the whole family. The most effective programs are comprehensive, well-planned, and long-lasting. Low-income children benefit the most.

- Interventions that strengthen family capacity to support learning and collaborate with teachers can improve low-income students' achievement and reduce achievement gaps.

A New Wave of Evidence: The Impact of School, Family, and Community Connections on Student Achievement (Henderson & Mapp, 2002) was published by the Southwest Educational Development Laboratory. Among its findings were:

- Higher-performing schools serving low-income families embraced a philosophy of partnership among teachers, families, and community members, and honored families' cultures and assets.

- Parent and community organizing to improve schools resulted in major successes: upgraded school facilities, improved leadership and staffing, higher-quality learning programs, and significant gains in student learning and graduation rates.

In this book, we have enlarged our frame of inquiry to:

1. Expand the evidence to consider impact and benefits not only to students, but also to educators, families, schools, and communities.

2. Identify policies, strategies, and practices that have high, even transformative impacts and benefits to all involved.

How Do We Define "Family Engagement"?

There are many definitions of family engagement, but little consistency in the field about what it means. We use this definition:

A full, equal, and equitable partnership among families, educators, and community partners to promote children's learning and development, from birth through college and career.

Here's some background on how it was developed. The Connecticut State Department of Education and the Office of Early Childhood decided to develop a definition of family engagement. The Commissioner's Roundtable on Family and Community Engagement—parent leaders, educators, policymakers, and community members—took on the task. Its goal was to co-develop a simple, useful definition. Participants worked in small groups, then shared their ideas with larger groups for input, over several cycles. Parents' views and experiences were captured in three rounds of focus groups. The final definition was presented for comment to a statewide symposium.

Parent and family leaders weighed in to explain what they meant by "full, equal, and equitable:"

- **Full:** Families, community partners, and educators work together as allies to promote children's learning and development. The goal is for all children to have high-quality learning opportunities *and* the supports they need to succeed.

- **Equal:** Families and educators bring equally valuable knowledge to the table. Parents know their children, culture, and community. Educators know curriculum and child development. Those understandings are complementary and essential to ensure success for all children.

- **Equitable:** Families are empowered to work with educators, public officials, and community partners to remove systemic and structural barriers that perpetuate inequities and injustice. This includes ready access to opportunities that develop their capacity to become full and equal partners (CT State Department of Education, 2018).

This definition of family engagement, which families and parent leaders influenced at each stage, was adopted in 2018 by the Connecticut State Department of Education, Office of Early Childhood and The Connecticut Council on Philanthropy. It now guides all state programs that serve children and families.

For real-life examples of what we mean by the concepts and terms defined on the following page, we turn to the Humphrey and Squires study that examined what happened when schools in the United Kingdom adopted Achievement for All (AfA), a program to improve outcomes for students with special needs (2011). A key component was hour-long "structured conversations about learning" between teachers and parents or another family member, held three times a year. During the conversation, parents and teachers spent time getting to know each other, shared insights about the student, co-developed a plan for improving learning, and settled on how they would stay in touch to monitor progress. In other words, they engaged in ***high-impact*** practices.

Families felt, often for the first time, that teachers listened to what they said about their children's interests and challenges, which bolstered their confidence. Teachers said they learned important things about their students and developed a new respect for parents. Students felt better understood and responded well to the supports their parents and teachers put in place. The conversations changed attitudes and beliefs, leading to a ***transformation*** in parent-teacher-student relationships.

The results of AfA were striking. Not only did the students in the program make greater gains than other students with special needs, but they also made greater gains than fellow students without special needs. Giving students the attention and support they needed led to more ***equitable*** outcomes that narrowed achievement gaps.

Key Concepts and Terms

In this section, we define several key concepts and terms that recur throughout the book.

Family: We use the word *family* instead of *parent* to recognize that all adult family members—siblings, grandparents, aunts, uncles, friends, and neighbors—contribute to a child's learning and development. If a study contains the word *parent*, however, we stick to it when describing the findings.

Nondominant: Nondominant families are those affected by systemic oppression, such as being marginalized based on race, class, language, or immigration status. This term explicitly references relationships to the dominant power structure. (Ishimaru, *Just Schools*, pg. 8). We use this term when referring to all families who have been marginalized or undervalued.

Multilingual: Many students are proficient in more than one language, even if they are not proficient in English. We acknowledge this as an asset by using the term *multilingual* instead of the phrases *English language learners* or *emergent bilingual*.

Engagement: Earlier editions from the Evidence series contained a variety of terms: *participation*, *involvement*, *connections*, and *engagement*. In this book, we also use *partnership*. Looking at this through the lens of courtship, we can see evolution: When we meet someone special, we *participate* in enjoyable activities together. As the relationship develops, we become *involved*. We make *connections* with our partner's friends and families and get to know them more deeply. If we become *engaged*, we commit to be

together for the rest of our lives. When we wed or enter a legally binding *partnership*, we make all important decisions together as equals.

High-impact: Traditional family engagement practices tend to have important, but minor, effects, such as a bump in test scores, school attendance, or homework completion. High-impact practices yield major, long-lasting effects. They improve students' academic outcomes, as well as their motivation, self-confidence, and agency. For example, contrast the tradition of sending home quarterly report cards with a set of practices where teachers meet each family face-to-face (in person or virtually), send home interactive learning materials, and regularly share progress via text message and folders of work. Combining high-impact practices like that can lead to:

Transformation: What we see in transformational change is a shift in beliefs and mindsets, from negative biases toward an appreciation of strengths and assets. That kind of change builds trust, which has pervasive and positive ripple effects on school culture. When relationships change from being cool, distant, and cautious to warm, collaborative, and inclusive, people work better together, and they enjoy each other's company more. Teacher morale improves. Students feel that being at school "is like being with family." This has a liberating effect on students, teachers, and families because it enables people to be who they are and bring their whole selves to the table.

Transformational change helps schools to become:

Equity-driven: By equity, we mean giving all children what they need to succeed. As a parent explained: "I have three children. One has Down Syndrome, one is super athletic, and the third is terribly shy. I love them all equally, but they need different things. If I treated them all the same, it wouldn't be fair." In schools that use high-impact practices, students receive the level of support and intervention that their needs require. The goal is a family-school partnership that enables all students to learn at high levels. To achieve that, power imbalances must be leveled so that everyone can contribute and be honored for what they bring.

How This Book Is Organized

We have organized this book to be easy to navigate. Chapters 1 to 4 focus on the impacts and benefits for all stakeholders. Each chapter poses questions addressed in the studies we reviewed and then identifies the high-impact practices that led to student gains, benefits for educators and families, transformation of school culture, and more equitable outcomes.

Chapter 1: Impact and Benefits to Students

- In what ways do children benefit when early childhood programs collaborate with families to support their learning?
- How can these benefits be sustained as children move through the K–12 school system?
- What family engagement practices have the most impact on student learning and development?
- How can engaging families help to turn around poor-performing schools?

Chapter 2: Impact and Benefits to Educators

- What benefits do educators experience from partnerships with families?
- How is their practice affected?
- What does effective educator-initiated family engagement practice look like?

Chapter 3: Impact and Benefits to Families

- In what ways does a family's sense of self-efficacy and personal development change depending on its relationships with those in the school?
- From the family's perspective, what elements are essential to develop strong relationships with teachers?
- What does the research tell us about the barriers to engagement that families experience?

Chapter 4: Impact and Benefits to Schools, Districts, and Communities

- How have families and communities contributed to systemic changes in their schools?
- How does family engagement factor into wider reform efforts?
- What steps can schools and districts take to elevate family engagement as a system-wide priority?
- What supports are necessary to create a culture of family-school partnership?

Chapter 5: Implications for Practice

This chapter integrates the major findings cited in this book with the *Dual Capacity-Building Framework for Family-School Partnerships* to show how they align and identifies major findings across the four core chapters. Then it proposes several recommendations for your practice based on the guiding principles that have emerged from our findings.

The Study Summaries

This section contains one-page summaries of the studies we reviewed, preceded by an alphabetical list of studies and a chart that organizes them by type of design. (Summaries are available for download at scholastic.com/EveryoneWinsResources.)

How We Selected the Studies

First, we identified possible candidates by contacting colleagues who do excellent research in the field, conducting a search on ERIC, and nominating studies we already knew about. Next, we reviewed the list to weed out studies that were out of date, not directly relevant, or had weak or inconclusive findings. Finally, we rated the studies using a three-star system. Studies that earned three stars have solid methodology, significant content, and useful detail about practices that lead to improved student outcomes and/or benefits for families, educators, schools, and/or communities. All the studies in this book rated three stars. This is by no means an all-inclusive list of worthy studies; we wish we had room to include more.

We are excited and inspired by the quality and diversity of this research. In the future, we hope our colleagues will include more student and family voices in their studies, and that the trend on identifying high-quality practice will continue.

Conclusion

Families know what their children need to ensure a good education that matches their hopes and dreams. When programs and practices follow the definition that parents helped craft and that we adopt earlier in this chapter, children do better in school, families gain confidence and leadership skills, teachers become effective collaborators, schools become engineers of equity, and communities develop a healthier, more cohesive, and more inclusive civic culture. In short: EVERYONE WINS! We hope that by reading this book, you and your school community will win, too.

CHAPTER 1

FAMILY ENGAGEMENT AND STUDENTS

Impact and Benefits

In a city in Great Britain, Samuel attends a small elementary school located amid public housing and blighted commercial property. Samuel could be disruptive in class and combative with his teachers. Sometimes he got into physical fights with schoolmates. At home, his mother often had trouble getting him to go to school.

During an hour-long "structured conversation," Samuel's mother explained to his teacher why her son was having these problems, notably a lack of contact with his father. She also informed the teacher that Samuel was being shunned by other students and had no friends to eat or play with. The teacher did not realize that troubling reality because she had not observed Samuel at lunch or recess.

Once she was aware of this, the teacher used an intervention called "Circle of Friends." When Samuel was out of the classroom, she explained to the rest of her students how people have different circles of helpers. Those helpers can include family members and close friends, as well as professionals, such as teachers and doctors. She asked the students if they wanted to be part of Samuel's circle of friends. Most members of the class volunteered. Each day Samuel could choose a few people from his circle to socialize with at lunch and recess, where his behavior had been at its worst.

Since the intervention began, Samuel has been far better behaved and has socialized with children who were previously afraid of him. He reports that getting feedback from his friends has been very useful. "Support from my friends has helped me improve my behavior. They tell me when I'm misbehaving" (Adapted from Humphrey & Squires, p. 90).

Text was sourced from the Department of Education, UK, and can be found on the gov.uk website.

What's in it for students? That basic question underlies all the research on family engagement. In this chapter, we start with the effects of family engagement on young children. From there, we move to elementary-age children to see whether and how the gains persist. Then we look at practices that sustain benefits for students, especially low-income students of color, as they move through middle and high school. Finally, we tackle the tough question of how to engage families to improve student learning in chronically low-performing schools.

As we move through the studies, you will see that strengthening the collaboration between families and school staff creates a cycle of positive interactions between parents and children. If sustained throughout a child's school years, those relationships predict healthy development, academic success, and a promising future.

The questions addressed by this collection of 14 studies are:

- In what ways do children benefit when early childhood programs collaborate with families to support their learning?
- How can those benefits be sustained as children move through the K–12 school system?
- What family engagement practices have the most impact on student learning and development?
- How can engaging families help to turn around poor-performing schools?

Looking across the studies, several big stories emerge:

1. Adding a family engagement component to early childhood programs improves children's outcomes.

2. Developing trust through close, equitable conversations between parents and teachers improves student achievement.

3. Collaborating with families through short-term interventions linked to learning can lead to significant gains in reading and math.

4. Partnering with secondary-school families improves student achievement, mental health, and graduation rates.

5. Using "radical healing" strategies helps students to resolve conflicts and promotes healthy relationships.

6. Collaborating with parents to remove structural inequities improves student outcomes.

In the sections that follow, we explore the findings that support each of these big stories about benefits, and identify the practices and conditions needed to make those benefits possible.

Big Story 1: Adding a family engagement component to early childhood programs improves children's outcomes.

Kindergarten readiness skills are a major predictor of children's school success. Early childhood programs with a strong family engagement component are more likely to help children reach that goal than programs without one. This includes giving families good information about child development, supporting them to reinforce learning at home, and building their skills to collaborate with teachers.

Another major predictor of future success is learning to read well. If early childhood programs extend their support for children and families through third grade, not only do students do better academically, they are also more likely to graduate from high school and go on to post-secondary learning. In addition, they are *less* likely to be mistreated, repeat a grade, require special education, or be arrested for a juvenile offense.

An excellent example is the Child-Parent Centers program in Chicago, which welcomes children from age three through third grade. In daily classes, young children engage in activities designed to promote academic and social success. A companion program supports families in promoting children's healthy development, connecting with other families, building relationships with teachers, connecting to community resources, and navigating the school system. Finally, program staff members facilitate children and families' transition into elementary school and provide support through third grade (Reynolds & Clements, 2005).

Build families' capacity to support learning and navigate the system.

In their long-term study, Reynolds and Clements (2005) found that children who started the CPC program at ages 3 or 4 had positive educational and social outcomes that continued up to 18 years after finishing the program. The longer their parents took part in CPC, the greater the benefits to children. For example: For each year a parent was involved in CPC, the likelihood of his or her child graduating from high school increased by 16 percent. That means that four years of involvement increased a child's odds of graduating high school by 48 percent.

The authors found that parents' participation in the CPC program contributed to children's development in three important ways:

1. Children's motivation, cognitive ability, social adjustment, and family and school support increased.

2. In turn, children's social competence, which included persistence, self-regulation, and positive relationships, also increased.

3. As a result, students had higher rates of school achievement and lower rates of grade retention, special education, delinquency, and need for social services.

> *In the past decade, two of the greatest advances in knowledge are that parent involvement in the education of low-income children helps explain the long-term effects of early childhood interventions, and that parent involvement in the elementary grades is associated with significantly higher rates of later educational attainment* (Reynolds & Clements, p. 122).

What Do Child-Parent Centers Look Like?

Parents visit CPC centers, which are based in schools or community settings, a half day per week, and can choose from a variety of activities. Here is what they find there:

- A Parent Resource Room, located in the CPC near the classrooms, with a full-time staff.
- A Parent-Resource Teacher who offers parent education and initiates interactions among parents and between parents and children.
- GED classes to help parents earn a high school credential.
- Fellow parents volunteering in children's classrooms, going on class field trips, preparing breakfasts and lunches, and engaging in education and training activities.
- A School Community Representative who conducts home visits and outreach to families.

Courtesy of © Human Capital Research Collaborative/cpcp3.org

Invest in family engagement over the long term.

Early in their lives, children tend to be optimistic, motivated, and eager to learn. Regrettably, those traits tend to fade the longer children are in school. How can that early receptivity be carried forward? We know that student motivation and academic achievement are linked. Does an increase in student motivation help explain the persistent influence of early parent involvement on later achievement?

Using Chicago CPC data, Hayakawa and her colleagues explored the connection between student motivation and parent involvement. They found that early parent involvement directly influenced kindergarten achievement, which in turn increased first-grade student motivation. Highly motivated children then encouraged their parents to continue their involvement. The benefits for CPC children were still evident at the end of sixth grade, when compared to a matched group of students who did not participate in CPC. (Hayakawa, Englund, Warner-Richter, & Reynolds, 2013).

To reduce the achievement gap in elementary school, the authors conclude that early interventions must aim to:

1. Begin reducing the gap early, in preschool and kindergarten.

2. Build in a mechanism for children to maintain higher achievement as they continue through elementary and secondary school.

Big Story 2: Developing trust through close, equitable conversations between parents and teachers improves student achievement.

Although traditional forms of family engagement such as volunteer programs, back-to-school nights, and parent-teacher conferences are useful, they are not designed to develop the trust that is essential for real partnership. We need to embrace practices that can transform the parent-teacher relationship. That means moving away from formal and reticent relationships, and toward wholehearted, equitable collaboration between partners who understand and respect each other.

The following studies show that deep conversations between teachers and parents allow three things to happen:

1. Teachers and parents share knowledge and insights about the child.

2. Teachers and parents affirm a mutual commitment to the child's success.

3. Teachers and parents develop a plan for working together to support the child's learning.

During these conversations, adults get to know and recognize each other as fully rounded human beings, which has a positive ripple effect on students, teachers, families, and schools:

- Students feel supported and reassured when the most important adults in their lives are working together to help them learn.

- Teachers obtain insights into their students' strengths and challenges, which helps them tailor instruction and spark interest.

- Families gain skills and confidence in helping their children learn and working within the school system.

- Schools become more welcoming and inclusive, which leads to more participation from families, changing the school climate in ways that benefit everyone.

Engage in close conversations to promote learning.

Developing an open, ongoing dialogue between teachers and parents about children's learning is central to Achievement for All (AfA), a program developed in the United Kingdom. In their study, Humphrey and Squires (2011) found that "structured conversations about learning" between teachers and parents was critical to AfA's success. The authors did not mince their words:

> *"This (structured conversation) strand of AfA was one of the resounding successes of the project for schools and parents alike. As one school declared, it has been 'the most powerful part of the project' and 'an absolute roaring success'"* (p. 58).

AfA has three main strands:

1. Assessment and tracking

2. "Wider outcomes" to ensure regular attendance and prosocial behavior

3. "Structured conversations" with parents to support learning

AfA targeted students with special educational needs and disabilities (SEND), which included students whose first language was not English and/or who were in foster care and/or eligible for free school meals. The program was piloted in 474 schools across the UK.

What Are Structured Conversations About Learning?

"Key teachers"—staff members who know students well and have regular contact with them—receive training in conducting "structured conversations." Each conversation lasts about an hour. AfA recommends that schools hold three conversations a year with the parents of each student, using a four-step model:

1. Develop a collaborative relationship and listen actively.

2. Focus on the critical skills the student needs to develop.

3. Co-develop a plan for collaborating.

4. Clarify next steps to move forward together.

Because these conversations are "human resource intensive," the authors strongly recommend that they should be embedded in school practice and faithfully implemented.

The study found that not only did parents become more engaged, but also that teachers deeply appreciated what they learned about their students from talking with parents. The gains for students were striking. SEND students in the AfA pilot made greater progress than SEND students nationally. In addition, AfA students in all grades except seventh made greater gains than the national average for all non-SEND students. (Chapter 2 contains a deeper discussion of the study on page 51.)

> *We were all a little bit skeptical at first… but once we got… the response from parents, (we) realized how much more information it was giving us, and what a better link it was creating. It was like the road to Damascus really… Why haven't we done this before? This is having such a major impact…. and it's not just with the child's individual development. It's this whole idea of liaison between home and school and making parents feel positive about what the school is doing for their child. Very much more this partnership role. So I think that's probably the biggest of all (Key Teacher, p. 56).*

The ripple effect is also striking: Not only did relationships between staff members and parents improve dramatically, but relationships between teachers and students improved as well.

Build trust with home visits.

The Parent-Teacher Home Visits (PTHV) project began in Sacramento, California, as an effort by community organizers to improve relationships between families and schools. Through one-on-one conversations and front-porch meetings, parents urged teachers to visit them in their home and find out who they really are.

Teachers visit homes in pairs—and only if the family has agreed to meet with them. All students in the class receive a visit; visits are *not* targeted to students who are struggling. Teachers are compensated for their time.

In the first home visit, usually in the fall, teachers focus on getting to know the family and building a positive relationship. By sharing their experiences, expectations, and goals for the child, they develop trust and mutual respect. From there, both parties discuss how they can collaborate to help the child reach those goals.

Sheldon and Jung (2018) examined the impact of home visits on students' academic progress and chronic absenteeism. The home visits seemed to have a positive effect on all students in the study, even if they didn't receive a home visit. For example, in schools that systematically visited at least ten percent of their students' families:

- Students were 22 percent *less likely* to be chronically absent.
- Students were 35 percent *more likely* to score "proficient" on ELA tests.

Both the AfA and PTHV studies strongly suggest that training teachers to have regular relationship-building conversations with families is critical. Working together to support students is a powerful strategy for improving their engagement, motivation, and performance. See other studies on PTHV on page 142 and page 153.

Big Story 3: Collaborating with families through short-term interventions linked to learning can lead to significant gains in reading and math.

With support from teachers, families can have a profound influence on their children's learning. An extensive review of research on young children revealed, across the board, that:

- Parents are eager for information on helping their children.

- With guidance, parents of all backgrounds can support learning at home.

- Children who took part in family engagement programs designed to improve their skills did significantly better in reading and math than children who didn't.

- Children do best when schools and community partners actively engage all families and make that engagement part of the "guiding philosophy" of their school or program.

- Sustained and targeted interventions are the most effective (Van Voorhis et al., 2013: *The Impact of Family Involvement on the Education of Children Ages 3 to 8*).

Secrets to Success in Reading and Math

 IN READING: Children made greater gains if they:

- Had more opportunities to engage in shared reading with family members.
- Interacted with parents in conversations and literacy-related activities.
- Got help from school volunteers.
- Had caring and competent teachers from preschool on (p. 49).

 IN MATH: Children's skills improved when their parents:

- Took part in targeted workshops that focused on well-designed homework activities.
- Engaged in those activities with their children.
- Used math games to build their children's essential math skills (p. 71).

What did not work for math?

- Suggesting without further explanation that parents get involved in impromptu math-related experiences that occur in daily life.
- "Homework as usual" that does not give family members opportunities to discuss math and how to apply it in the real world (p. 71).

(Van Voorhis et al., 2013)

Parents from diverse backgrounds, when given direction, can become more engaged with their children on literacy and math activities—and their children can increase their reading and math skills, on average, more so than children whose parents are operating without support or direction (p. ES-3).

See high gains with light-touch, low-tech approaches.

Communicating with families using SMS messaging on a mobile phone might be useful at any time. But it's critical during disruptions that require children to learn remotely, such as during the COVID-19 pandemic. Children can make significant gains in reading and math if the messages:

- Support home learning.

- Link explicitly to what children are learning and doing in class.

- Invite two-way communication about how the child is doing.

- Are written in families' home languages.

For example, Keith Welch studied pre-K and kindergarten teachers who were using FASTalk, a text-messaging system designed to enhance parent-teacher communication. Messages about literacy learning went home three times a week for eight weeks. All messages were linked to the school's curriculum and translated into each family's home language. Not only did FASTalk students outpace a matched comparison group, but students whose parents took part more often and students whose first language was not English made even greater gains (Welch, 2018).

Take results up a notch with the personal touch.

In Botswana, Africa, researchers evaluated a trial program using SMS text messaging when schools closed in March 2020. Over 4,500 households participated. One group received weekly SMS messages with several simple math problems. The other group received the same weekly messages, followed by a personal phone call to provide support, motivation, and accountability. A third group served as the control. Students in both SMS groups made marked improvements on a standardized math test, but gains in the second group were nearly twice as high. Most families wanted to continue the program, with a high demand for messages plus phone calls (Angrist et al., 2020).

Add value by building capacity in both teachers and families.

Springboard Summer, a five-week summer program for elementary students, works to reverse summer learning loss and to cultivate successful reading habits, centering families to make that happen. Families attend workshops on supporting their children's literacy that built their capacity as fellow educators with expertise about their children. In turn, teachers receive training on engaging families effectively. In a study of five school districts, Springboard Summer "scholars" in grades K–4 made significant improvement. Students who began the program below grade level had the largest gains (Piccinino et al., 2020).

Springboard Summer uses a three-pronged approach:

- **For scholars:** A five-part literacy block (read-aloud, shared reading, word work, differentiated reading in literacy centers, and writing) as well as achievement incentives.
- **For families:** Initial home visits and weekly family workshops on how to support reading.
- **For teachers:** Training and coaching to improve instruction and family engagement skills.

Combine text messages with personal calls to develop productive relationships among teachers, parents, and students.

To evaluate the connections between teacher-parent communication, teacher-student communication, and student outcomes, Kraft and Dougherty (2013) conducted an experiment. They assigned a group of sixth- and ninth-grade students attending a mandated summer school program to receive a *daily* text message from teachers while their parents receive a *daily* phone call from teachers. They found that those frequent teacher-parent communications produced three immediate effects. Students were more likely to:

1. participate in class discussions and activities.
2. remain on task, without teacher prompting.
3. complete homework.

Those daily family-teacher communications also improved student engagement. Why? The authors provide three reasons:

Stronger teacher-student relationships: Calling and texting home led to a better rapport between teachers and students, increasing student motivation to learn. It also helped teachers manage the classroom more effectively.

Expanded parent involvement: Calling and texting home helped parents understand their child's academic progress and behavior. With the information calls and texts provided, parents could hold their children accountable for their actions and efforts at school, as well as better support their academic achievement.

Increased student motivation: As a result of support from teachers and parents, students were more motivated to perform well in class, which complements the findings of Reynolds and Clements's CPC studies (2005) and Hayakawa et al. (2016). In contrast to those studies, however, Kraft and Dougherty investigated short-term interventions. We do not know for how long the positive results lasted once the interventions were over.

Big Story 4: Partnering with secondary-school families improves student achievement, mental health, and graduation rates.

What should family engagement look like as children enter adolescence and the more complicated structures of middle and high schools? What role should families play as their children are becoming more independent? Who in the school knows their children well and can serve as a point person if a problem arises? Do family members have a voice in selecting their children's program and supporting their success? How can they partner with counselors and staff members to guide their children toward post-secondary education and a meaningful career? Several studies shed light on those burning questions.

Balance support and independence.

In their literature review, Jensen and Minke (2017) found that higher rates of family engagement in high school benefit students in several ways. Not only did academic achievement and graduation rates increase, but rates of anxiety, depression, and aggression decreased. Instead of helping students with homework, parents shifted to advising and coaching, emphasizing the importance of education and goal-setting. The researchers call this "academic socialization." Family engagement also strengthened the parent-child relationship, students' sense of efficacy and self-esteem, and parents' sense that their students welcomed their support.

> *"There is no inherent conflict in a focus on parent engagement in secondary schools and a focus on fostering competence and self-reliance among adolescents"* (p. 182).

What supports should high schools provide for families to remain engaged? Jensen and Minke identified several:

- Explain to families how the school is organized, how it monitors progress, and what programs are available.

- Provide transition services for students and their families as they enter the school.

- Help students and families plan for college and careers after graduation.

- Offer professional development to teachers on how to engage families more effectively.

- Employ a family-school liaison or parent-engagement facilitator who is familiar with the cultural backgrounds of the families served.

- Provide information on adolescent development and how to balance students' growing self-reliance with continued family support.

- Plan interventions to ensure equitable engagement between educators and families, rather than "top-down" interventions from one side or the other.

Help students and families transition between middle and high school.

Offering a middle-to-high-school transition program can make a big difference since adjusting to a more complex school environment, such as high school, often requires extra support. Ninth grade is a critical year; failing one or two subjects can derail a student's chances of graduation. This problem is compounded by the fact that, as their children age, parents struggle to stay connected to daily life at school. The good news is that middle and high schools can partner with families to help students successfully navigate the transition and stay engaged through high school graduation.

A study of middle- to high-school transition programs by researchers from the National Network of Partnership Schools (NNPS) found that the extent to which students struggle academically was highly related to two factors:

1. The quality of the schools' transition program, if the school even had one.

2. The number of parents who were able to guide their children's learning.

Schools serving low-income communities were less likely to have strong transition programs and more likely to have students having difficulty. Across the sample, however, high schools that made a serious effort to include parents in the transition process—including schools in high-poverty areas—had significantly fewer ninth graders falling behind in their classes (MacIver, Epstein, Sheldon, & Fonseca, 2015).

Successful Transition Practices to High School

- Invite incoming students and parents to visit the school before the new school year begins.

- Communicate with parents before the start of the year about the school's expectations for students' attendance, behavior, and achievement.

- Suggest ways that families can support their child's transition to high school.

- Communicate with parents throughout the year on how to monitor their child's progress.

- Inform parents about the school's family engagement program, including the NNPS Action Team for Partnerships.

- Collaborate with feeder schools to prepare students and families to move on to the next level.

(MacIver et al., 2015)

Work with families to give all students the support they need to succeed.

Secondary schools that provide pathways to college or career preparation programs for all students, with data-informed structures to support struggling students, rigorous academic programs, a college-going culture, and close collaboration with families, can beat the odds.

Carol Ascher and Cindy Maguire (2007) studied 13 higher-performing high schools—or the Beating the Odds Schools—in New York City, serving nearly 100 percent students of color from low-income families. All the schools had graduation rates that were 10 points above the NYC district average.

The effort began at the start of ninth grade with student and family orientation meetings. Throughout the year, parent coordinators (often students' family members or alumni of the school) facilitated "parent academies" on evenings and weekends to help families fill out complicated financial aid and college or post-secondary program application forms. As an English teacher who helps students with their essays and prep for the New York State Regents' Examination put it, "Whatever needs to be done, we step up to do it."

The table on the next page provides examples of the various practices that BTO schools used to engage families. For more information on this study, see page 119.

> *"What matters most is high academic expectations, a quality instructional program, extra academic support, and regular contact between students and adults."*
>
> —High school students, NYC Urban Youth Collaborative

By the time their children reach ninth grade, most parents have become less involved at school. Students often say they want their parents to back off. To make matters more challenging, schools often send the message that "it's time to let go," leaving families unsure about what they're supposed to do. Clearly, parents need help navigating a complex secondary system and guiding their children through it successfully.

The more that educators keep parents informed about what their children are studying, how well they are doing, what is required for them to graduate, and how to plan for post-secondary education, the more effectively parents can guide their children. This research shows that engaging families through high school is critical to students' staying in school, taking more challenging classes, graduating on time, and going to college or a postsecondary program.

Beating the Odds: Components of an Effective Program to Engage High School Families

Feature/Purpose	Vision	Examples of Practices
TRANSITION PROGRAM: Help students and families make the adjustment to high school	Key message: This is a college-prep high school! We'll work with you to make sure your student makes it.	• Events at feeder schools to welcome families, followed by tours of the high school • Summer bridge program to prep students for high-school-level work, explain the school's academic program • Workshops for families
ADVISORY SYSTEM: Each student has an adult advisor who is the family's key contact.	Every student has at least one adult in the school he, she, or they can count on.	• Meetings with family, starting in ninth grade, to draw up plan for future, select an academic program to match • Regular information to family about student's program, learning opportunities
PROCESS TO MONITOR PROGRESS: Families can expect a regular, two-way flow of information.	No student will fall through the cracks.	• Clear and explicit sequence of information, from ninth to twelfth grade • Regular exhibits of student work • End-of-year assessments, with adjustments to program for following year
COLLEGE/POST-SECONDARY INFORMATION: Families get info they need directly from the school.	All students will apply to college or a post-secondary program and for financial aid.	• College/post-secondary program awareness starting at the beginning of ninth grade • Plan for college begun by end of ninth grade • Exposure to colleges and programs via fairs and visits • Test prep, including Regents Exam (or equivalent) • Financial aid guidance
STRONG PARENT ORGANIZATION: Parents get info out to other families.	Parent voice is essential to good decisions.	• Parent organization and leadership that represent all families in the school • Parent leaders who sit on college-pathways and school-leadership teams • Parent organization that conducts focus groups with families to surface issues and concerns

Big Story 5: Using "radical healing" strategies helps students to resolve conflicts and promotes healthy relationships.

Bringing young people together to recover from trauma, identify a vision for their schools and communities, and take action to implement that vision is a recipe for collective well-being. This approach differs from programs such as trauma-informed care because it addresses what is causing the trauma in the first place, such as racism, structural inequity, classism, and unconscious bias, which have toxic effects on young people.

When we talk about family engagement, we mean the whole family, including students. In high school, as students are becoming young adults, their voices, experiences, and opinions increasingly need to be considered. They are an integral part of the family engagement equation. Ginwright's research centers on students, but always situates them as members of families and the school community.

What Is Radical Healing?

Radical healing is a process to restore hope in traumatized young people by empowering them to create and carry out a vision of well-being for themselves and their school. Shawn Ginwright recommends three steps in the process:

1. **Recognize signs of collective and individual harm.** Pay attention to our own and others' social emotional states. Healing circles that bring young people together with teachers and parents to have honest conversations are a good way to start.

2. **Define what well-being looks like in a school.** How might well-being shape strategies to reduce violence and promote peaceful conflict resolution? Push for what *can* exist, rather than what *does* exist.

3. **Implement practices that facilitate healing and infuse well-being and joy.** For example: Integrate families' cultural practice into school rituals, reflect on root causes of issues, identify ways to act on those issues, encourage students to share their stories, talk about what gives life meaning, and celebrate victories both large and small (Ginwright, 2016, p. 129).

Foster well-being.

Students in distressed communities respond well to healing strategies designed to create schools that foster well-being. How can educators respond to hopelessness in ways that restore human dignity, meaning, and possibility?

In his book, *Hope and Healing in Urban Education* (2016), Shawn Ginwright describes efforts in several high schools in the San Francisco Bay Area to reduce conflict. Leaders at those schools developed a vision for changing course and brought students, parents, teachers, and administrators together to discuss how to make it happen.

The effects were dramatic. In 2007, Restorative Justice for Oakland Youth (RJOY) began supporting about 30 schools to reduce suspension rates and increase academic achievement. By 2014, RJOY schools had achieved an 87 percent reduction in suspensions (p. 99).

Engage in critical inquiry.

Ginwright found that a key strategy for school success is forming a voluntary "critical inquiry group" of teachers and administrators interested in learning about healing from trauma, racism, and culturally responsive teaching. Facilitated by teachers, this group allowed participants to reflect on the impact of racism and unconscious bias on student performance. Then members discussed how to improve their teaching and healing practices.

Once teachers put those practices into action and established more trusting and respectful relationships with students and families, the culture in their classrooms changed as students and teachers began to deepen their connections. Acts of sharing, listening, and affirming allowed relationships to develop that do *not* flourish when teaching focuses strictly on mastering content. Some strategies teachers used were:

- Connecting learning to students' daily experiences.
- Holding morning "community circles" to check in and set the tone for the day and week.
- Affirming and celebrating local cultural traditions.
- Encouraging trust, honesty, and vulnerability during lessons.
- Sharing the teachers' own experiences and challenges with students.
- Nurturing relationships outside the classroom with students' family.

The improved teacher-student relationship brought benefits to both. When teachers better understood students and their family circumstances, they were more effective in engaging their students, enriching the content of instruction, and integrating students' experiences into classroom lessons. Ginwright found that teachers began to see themselves as part of a community, not just a school, and took on a more familial role with students. Teachers also reported a deeper sense of purpose and clarity about themselves and about their work. The story below illustrates how students respond.

Relational Pedagogy in Action

"Relational pedagogy" means integrating students' daily lives into class lessons. In an Oakland high school history class, Ms. Jennings was leading a discussion about Día de los Muertos, an important Latin American holiday. Students had made masks symbolizing someone important to them. Sitting in a circle, they took turns explaining their masks. They shared stories of loss and pain, violence at home and in the streets.

One student explained, "I haven't seen my dad since I was eight years old. He went to jail…. The bars right here on the mask represent where my dad is, and this basketball … reminds me when we used to play basketball when I was younger."

The masks were more than masks. They were a portal that gave students permission to be honest and vulnerable. In stark contrast to other classes where those same students were often bored and disruptive, in Ms. Jennings's class they listened intently. Ms. Jennings said, "When we do lessons like this, I always look for opportunities for students to share and listen to each other. I think we build trust when we do that, and they learn a lot because the lessons are real for them!" (Ginwright, 2016, p. 103).

Ginwright's research focuses on the effects on young people when adults in the school listen to them, find ways to heal their pain, and empower them to improve the conditions that have caused trauma. Although parents are also engaged in this work, students are at the center. This is essential, because to become confident, independent adults, students must find their voice. That can happen only if caring adults listen to students and heed what they say.

Big Story 6: Collaborating with parents to remove structural inequities improves student outcomes.

Chronic underachievement in schools serving low-income neighborhoods is a vexing reality. Underlying structural inequities severely limit opportunities and resources for students. But what happens when families team up with community organizations to take action to improve schools? This, too, is family engagement. Organized parents have won major victories using "tools of democracy" such as attending open meetings, demonstrating peacefully, holding "accountability sessions" with public officials, and attracting press coverage. Their efforts have led to improved facilities, better curriculum, higher-quality programs, and more qualified teachers (Mediratta, Shah, & McAlister, 2009; Warren, Mapp et al. *A Match on Dry Grass*, 2011).

Provide leadership training for parents, teachers, and administrators together.

The work of Austin Interfaith, a community-organizing group in Austin, Texas, is a good example of reducing structural inequities. In addition to parents and community members, it welcomes local religious congregations and Education Austin, the teachers' union. When its work began, nearly half the district's 70,000 students qualified for the free and reduced-price lunch program. Only about 60 percent of them met the minimum standards on the Texas Assessment of Academic Skills (TAAS).

Over eight years, Austin Interfaith created a network of "Alliance Schools" made up of nearly half the district's high-poverty schools. In those schools, its organizers provided leadership training to parents, teachers, and administrators and supported them in implementing reforms to improve student learning. The group also developed effective relationships with the superintendent and several school board members.

> *Reinventing the culture of schools was a radical idea. Before becoming involved in Austin Interfaith, the idea of neighbors changing schools did not make sense. The word* power *was not in my vocabulary.*
> —Lourdes Zamarron, parent leader (p. 11)

As described in a multi-method case study by Mediratta, Shah, and McAlister, those efforts led to profound changes in the district's priorities, the schools' capacity for improvement, and the students' academic progress. Intensity of involvement in Alliance Schools activities predicted increases in students' TAAS scores, which ranged from a four-point increase in schools with minimal involvement to a 15–19-point increase in schools with high involvement (2009, p. 29).

Parents and community organizers working together created major change.

When parents at Zavala Elementary School learned their school was the lowest performing in Austin based on TAAS scores, they were furious. And low attendance of the students and teachers wasn't helping the matter. So, the principal reached out to Austin Interfaith organizers for help. To start, Austin Interfaith organized a team of parents, teachers, and administrators for a "neighborhood walk," during which they visited homes to talk with families about how things were going and what needed to change.

Working with the team, Austin Interfaith organizers analyzed information gathered from neighborhood walks and other sources. Based on its findings, the team introduced a slate of reforms for the following school year:

- New curricula in language arts and math
- A school-based clinic to provide health care for students
- An accelerated science program
- An inclusion policy to teach special education students in regular classrooms
- More planning time for teachers
- A new after-school program

Within two years, attendance of both students and teachers improved and the TAAS scores rose. (Mediratta et al., *Building Partnerships to Reinvent School Culture: Austin Interfaith*, p. 8.)

In districts with chronically underperforming schools, a higher level of intervention is required to improve the situation. "Reinventing" the culture by introducing community organizing strategies united Zavala parents, teachers, and administrators. Starting there allowed the school community to avoid laying blame and share a common purpose.

Building community starts with listening. To create consensus about what needed to happen, parents, teachers, and administrators embarked on a listening campaign through neighborhood walks and house meetings. The understandings they gained transformed the way they saw each other, moving away from stereotypes and bias. That, in turn, profoundly altered the way they understood their respective roles in school improvement and, consequently, how they worked together as a school community. To achieve shared goals, they learned to share power for the benefit of students.

Conclusion

Providing a seamless pathway for families to navigate the school system from pre-K through high school is essential to keeping students on track. What does that look like? The journey begins with early childhood educators partnering with families to address learning delays, prepare children for kindergarten, develop reading skills, and help parents understand how the system works. The passage continues with school teams providing children and families with smooth transitions from preschool to elementary school to middle school to high school and beyond, and clearly explaining the programs and expectations that lie ahead.

Close collaboration between families and educators along the way includes home visits, extended conversations about learning, and constant communication through email, Internet portals, SMS text messaging, and social media. Planning for post-secondary education and careers starts in middle school. Students tend to succeed when they are prepared to take the courses and programs in high school that align with their goals. Many will need constant coaching, mental health support, and academic assistance from teachers, families, and community organizations. High schools with college and career centers that provide information and guidance to the whole family have the greatest impact on students' future success.

Investing in programs like the ones described in this chapter that help students and families navigate the school system successfully is a delectable recipe for cost-effective success. The next chapters cover the impact and benefits to teachers, families, schools, and communities of partnering with families to promote their children's learning and well-being.

CHAPTER 2

FAMILY ENGAGEMENT AND EDUCATORS

Impact and Benefits

When Robert Cordova, a seasoned educator and the principal at Harmony Elementary School in South Central Los Angeles, explains his initial involvement with the IAF, he does it as crisply as he dresses—in freshly pressed suits and neatly cuff-linked shirts. He begins his story with his first year as principal at City Terrace Elementary School in East Los Angeles. There he faced "pesky parents," a group that was quite vocal in its criticisms of the school. Taking those criticisms seriously, Cordova began to search for successful educational systems that were working for and with Latino populations similar to his. He discovered the Alliance Schools in Texas:

> I was investigating some of the schools in Texas that had some real success and... some of them were IAF Alliance Schools... and I said, well, I'm going to investigate this and I went to some of the IAF trainings and began to learn their strategy of working with the community, not just the parents... I started to do it and I saw the power.

While participating in IAF trainings in Texas, Cordova encountered Alliance Schools' principals, and he knew almost immediately that he wanted to work as effectively with his community as they were working with theirs. "You can do these other things, you can make yourself look good, and you can get promoted, but are you really going to do something that's meaningful? Are you really going to have the power to do something that is meaningful?" To determine what "meaningful" work might look like in his school, Cordova began listening to parents in a new way—learning about their interests in, concerns about, and hopes and dreams for their children. With mentoring and guidance of One LA, a community organizing network, Cordova got City Terrace parents, teachers, and community members talking in purposeful ways to discover their shared concerns for the children's well-being.

Intentional listening deepened trust among all participants. As a result, relationships became stronger and provided a basis for building power and influence. It was not long before parents, teachers, and community members convinced the city to install a traffic sign at a dangerous intersection that students and families had to cross while walking to and from school. That early victory inspired parents, teachers, and community members and made them confident that, together, they could make positive change in their community. It convinced Cordova that true leadership begins with building the trust of parents, teachers, and community members by mobilizing around their shared interests and concerns for their children, school, and community (Adapted from Warren & Mapp, 2011, pp. 84, 85).

Historically, much of the research on the impact of family-school partnerships has centered on their impact on student outcomes. In this chapter, we shift the conversation to focus on their impact on *educators*—the teachers, school and district leaders, and other staff and program personnel—who work as practitioners in schools and educational programs.

Why is presenting the impact of family engagement on educators important?

In 1984, the fast-food chain Wendy's introduced a commercial featuring Clara Peller, the feisty senior citizen who asked her now-famous question, "Where's the beef?" Clara's question has come to represent a phrase used in the decades since the commercial's release to ask about outcomes and accountability—and is precisely what many educators wonder when asked to spend time and attention on building partnerships with families: Where's the beef? What's in it for me?

This collection of studies seeks to answer that question by showcasing the "wins" for educators who partner with families. While reviewing the studies, we sought answers to the following questions:

- What benefits do educators experience from partnerships with families?

- How do those partnerships affect their practice?

- What does effective or high-impact family engagement look like?

From the 15 studies we reviewed, five big stories emerged:

1. Building partnerships with families activates shifts in educators' beliefs and mindsets.

2. Engaging in partnerships with families shifts educators' practice.

3. Cultivating and nourishing family partnerships leads to a positive school culture and retention of staff.

4. Sustaining meaningful family engagement requires certain skills, mindsets, and dispositions.

5. Supporting effective family engagement requires resources, leadership, and infrastructure.

Big Story 1: Building partnerships with families activates shifts in educators' beliefs and mindsets.

In his book, *Fire in the Heart*, Mark Warren chronicles the journey of 50 White activists for racial justice (2010). Forty-six of the activists interviewed by Warren described experiencing a moment, an event, or an incident that was a "profound moral shock," forever altering their sense of race and the reality of racism in the United States. This "seminal experience" served as the catalyst for a change in their beliefs and mindsets about justice and equity, and permanently shaped their strategies and actions going forward (p. 24).

"Seminal experience" is a recurring theme in the studies on the impact of family engagement on educators in this chapter. That experience, usually a moment in a conversation, during a relationship-building event, or during a learning opportunity between educators and families, activates in educators a different way of thinking and feeling about families. It sparks a transformation of beliefs about the benefits and power of family engagement and a shift in how they engage with families.

Educators shift beliefs and mindsets about who families are.

When educators take advantage of relational opportunities with families—occasions when educators and families get to share information and learn and value each other's stories— educators' beliefs about families shift.

In Chapter 1, we discussed the positive impact of home visits on students. What about the impact of those visits on educators? In their 2017 qualitative study of the Parent-Teacher Home Visits (PTHV) model, Katherine McKnight and her colleagues examined whether and how PTHV interrupted implicit biases that educators and families had about each other. The authors looked at three main sources of data:

1. The research literature on implicit biases

2. A field scan of other home-visit programs

3. Qualitative data collected from schools in each of four large districts that were conducting PTHV.

What's the Difference Between a Belief and a Mindset?

Belief: something that is accepted, considered to be true, or held as an opinion

Mindset: a way of being; a mental attitude or inclination

Schools in the study served mostly students of color and from low-income families. The researchers interviewed the school leaders and conducted focus groups with educators and families at each school, totaling 175 participants.

The study findings revealed that, when educators listened to and engaged with families, they realized that any negative assumptions and beliefs they held about families were unfounded. They also called into question any assumptions they held about families lacking the capacity to support their children's learning and needing their help and guidance. One teacher shared how PTHV altered her deficit-based beliefs and mindsets about families:

What Is Implicit Bias?

Thoughts and feelings are "implicit" if we are unaware of them or mistaken about their nature. We have a bias when we have a preference for (or aversion to) a person or group of people. Thus, we use the term "implicit bias" to describe the tendency to hold attitudes toward people, or to stereotype them, without being conscious of doing it. (Perception Institute: perception.org/research/implicit-bias/)

> *What I thought in my infinite wisdom was that I was going to go in, and I was going to see my impoverished families with no books and no focused learning time and no outside positive influences. I had this bizarre kind of belief of what went on in my homes. Once I got into our homes, 95 percent of them are incredible. I'm seeing culture and I'm seeing a love of education. I'm seeing a love of family, and all those preconceived ideas are going by the wayside. I always felt... well, that they needed us, to show them the way. That's not true. We could learn a lot from our families, and we needed to value their experience and we needed to value what they brought rather than what we could do for them, which was where I was coming from.*
>
> —PTHV teacher (p. 14–15)

PTHV challenged and ultimately reframed this teacher's "bizarre kind of belief" about families.

After conducting a few PTHVs, educators began to see the assets and "funds of knowledge" (Moll, 2019) that families brought to school—and began to learn and benefit from them. The researchers referred to these interruptions of biases as "mindset shifts," and hypothesized that those shifts might enable educators and families to partner more effectively to support student success.

Educators redefine family engagement—and rethink its value and importance.

What is the difference between family involvement and family engagement? The educator and author Larry Ferlazzo describes it this way:

> *A school striving for family involvement often leads with its mouth—identifying projects, needs, and goals and then telling parents how they can contribute. A school striving for [family] engagement, on the other hand, tends to lead with its ears—listening to what parents think, dream, and worry about. The goal of family engagement is not to serve clients but to gain partners* (2009).

Several of the studies we reviewed emphasize this shift from involvement to engagement. For example, for their study on barriers to engagement, Baker, Wise, Kelley, and Skiba (2016) conducted focus groups with parents and staff at six schools (three elementary, two middle, and one high school) in a Midwestern state. They created 20 focus groups containing 50 parents and 76 staff members.

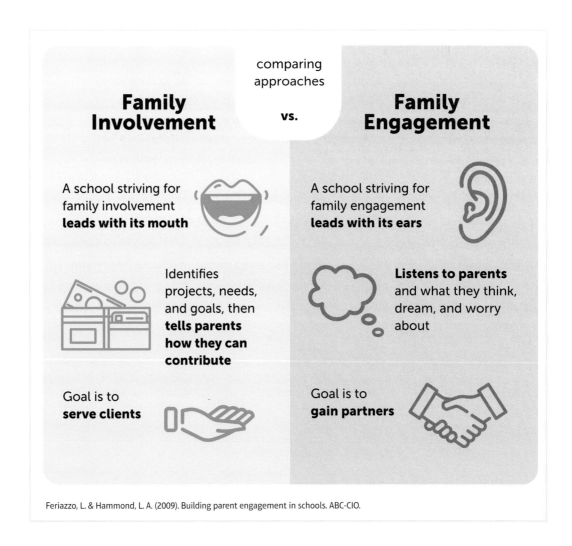

comparing approaches

Family Involvement vs. **Family Engagement**

A school striving for family involvement **leads with its mouth**

A school striving for family engagement **leads with its ears**

Identifies projects, needs, and goals, then **tells parents how they can contribute**

Listens to parents and what they think, dream, and worry about

Goal is to **serve clients**

Goal is to **gain partners**

Ferlazzo, L. & Hammond, L. A. (2009). Building parent engagement in schools. ABC-CIO.

The researchers defined parent *involvement* as the focus on parents being present in the schools and defined parent *engagement* as the "intentional efforts by the school to recognize and respond to parents' voices and to help school staff to better understand how to address barriers that parents have identified" (p. 163). Each focus group was asked these two questions:

- What are the barriers or limitations to families attending school events?

- What can be done differently to increase family involvement?

Findings revealed that parents and staff members identified similar barriers, such as childcare, feeding families before events, and work constraints, but the two parties offered contrasting solutions:

- Parents asked for solutions that moved beyond the school building and engaged them at home or in the community, with activities that supported their children's education.

- Unlike the parents, who had a wider view of what parent engagement could look like, staff members offered solutions that required parent *involvement* in the school itself. They were more inclined to have parents attend school events consistently rather than thinking through other forms of engagement.

The researchers state:

> *Schools should embrace a more expansive view of parent engagement, which includes multiple constructions of how parents are involved. Parents who may have too many competing obligations or responsibilities to be able to consistently be present at the school are looking for alternatives and for school staff who value their input and participation outside the school building. Moving from parent presence to engagement may require a profound attitude shift that focuses on the strengths and resources that families can bring to their child's education* (Peña, 2000) *and intentional and consistent attention to addressing barriers with connected solutions* (p. 180).

Ann Ishimaru (2019) pushes even deeper our thinking about the differences between family involvement and true collaborations with families and communities. She conducted a study of three initiatives designed to engage families and communities in their children's education. Specifically, she looked at two school-based initiatives and one neighborhood-based initiative, within a cross-sector collaboration network consisting of schools and various community organizations in a Western region of the United States that sought to improve family engagement.

Using an equity-based conceptual framework she developed for her earlier empirical work, with some community-organizing theory woven in, Ishimaru distinguishes the "rules of engagement" between traditional involvement-based partnerships and more equitable collaborations. The chart below identifies the various goals, strategies, parent roles, and contexts.

Contrasting Rules of Engagement Between Partnerships and Equitable Collaborations

	Traditional Partnerships	Equitable Collaborations
Goals	Material resources and discrete aims within a culture of denial or implicit blame	Systemic change within a culture of shared responsibility
Strategies	Inside, technical change	Adaptive change to build capacity and relationships of a broad range of stakeholders
Parent role	Nondominant parents as clients and beneficiaries (educators/ professionals set the agenda)	Nondominant parents as educational leaders who contribute and help shape the agenda
Context	Apolitical approach focused on schools in isolation	Reform as a political process that addresses broader issues in community

Ishimaru's framework goes further by identifying the differences in the intervention level, directionality of the relationship, and the power dynamics between traditional partnerships and equitable collaborations:

Dimensions of Equitable Collaboration Strategies That Build Capacity and Relationships

Dimension	Traditional Partnerships	Equitable Collaborations
Intervention level	Individual parent/student	Collective families/communities
Directionality Power	Unidirectional Unilateral	Reciprocal Relational

Ishimaru found that, although the parent/family capacity-building strategies in practice did engage families in more equitable ways, many of the strategies mirrored educator-defined agendas and expectations for parent behavior, maintaining top-down school dynamics and power relations.

This study suggests that articulating and embracing new beliefs and mindsets about "involvement vs. engagement" is necessary, but not sufficient to disrupt long-held traditional practices. In an earlier study, Ishimaru (2014) found that powerful "institutional scripts"—those long held mindsets about who should have power and authority and the proper roles for families and for school staff—often stand in the way of equitable collaboration and engagement. Both studies make clear that shifting from an involvement to an engagement mindset requires focus and determination.

Big Story 2: Engaging in partnerships with families shifts educators' practice.

Changing the way educators define engagement and think about partnering with families is critical, but real possibilities for partnership emerge when they move from just *thinking* differently about engagement to permanently *transforming* their practice.

In particular, both teachers and school leaders are able to shift how they communicate with families and integrate families' wisdom and knowledge into their practice. Here, we discuss how they do that.

Shifts in the Practice of Teachers

The Humphrey and Squires (2011) study described in Chapter 1 highlights how teachers changed their communication with families and integrated what they learned into their practice. Specifically, it explored the effects of the Achievement for All (AfA) program, which was designed to improve outcomes for students with special educational needs and disabilities (SEND). One of the components of the program was "structured conversations," where teachers were trained to have an open dialog with families, and asked to have three conversations a year with parents of SEND students, using a four-step model:

1. **Explore** (e.g., active listening): To develop a collaborative relationship

2. **Focus** (e.g., identify priorities): To support developing critical skills

3. **Plan** (e.g., agree on targets): To co-develop a plan for collaborating

4. **Review** (e.g., clarify next steps): To move forward together

The researchers, as well as those they interviewed for the study, felt that the structured conversations strand of the intervention was the most successful. Not only did they find that family engagement improved, but also that teachers deeply appreciated what they learned about their students from talking with parents. For some schools, the three conversations per year allowed educators and parents to formulate a joint working agreement in which they could plan and map student progress throughout the year (p. 56).

The conversations allowed teachers to focus on students' achievements, rather than their shortcomings, which are typically raised in meetings with parents. Teachers found that they had time to listen to parents rather than just talk, which resulted in greater understanding of each other's perspectives. At one school, the structured conversations were renamed "listening conversations" to reflect that welcome result. One teacher stated:

> There have been changes in the way we work. I think particularly in the way of gaining the views of parents, starting with the views of parents as opposed to the school thrusting the agenda. Trying to get a gauge of where their thinking is and what they feel their children need.... They're taking more of an ownership, and it's written down.... They can look back and see what targets their child's being set (AfA Lead, School 10, LA E, p. 59).

The McKnight et al. study (2017), which was described earlier in this chapter, also found that educators incorporated what they learned from home visits into their teaching strategies. One teacher stated:

> So, if I know that their dad works in construction, I can... when we're talking about area and perimeter, we can talk about when you're building a house, you need to make sure you're measuring accurately. And then you need to calculate the square footage of a floor to be able to figure out how much flooring you need. Or you need to figure out volume to figure out how much concrete you need to pour a foundation. And when they're like, "Whoa! My dad uses this. Maybe I should actually learn this" (PTHV teacher, p. 22).

Shifts in the Practice of School Leaders

When school leaders were exposed to and experimented with meaningful models of engagement, they, too, changed their practice. In their study, Warren and Mapp (2011) explored the methods, processes, and capacities through which community organizing works to create and support equity- and justice-oriented school reform. One key finding revealed the transformative effect that community organizing had on educators, community leaders, and policy makers who collaborated with families, students, and community members.

For school leaders, participating in meetings with families, where they were able to hear concerns and suggestions and learn about the tools of organizing, shifted their beliefs about families and their mindsets about engaging with them. Being exposed to new and different ways of communicating and working with families presented new opportunities for school leaders and staff.

As we read in the vignette that began this chapter, Robert Cordova went from being a principal who referred to a group of vocal families at his first school as "pesky parents" to a leader who embraced families as valuable partners. As a result of his investigation of the Industrial Areas Foundation (IAF) Alliance Schools initiative in Texas, his role in organizing trainings, and the wisdom he gleaned from Alliance Schools principals, Cordova made relational organizing central to his leadership, "building trust with parents and teachers by mobilizing around their shared interests and concerns for their children, school, and community" (p. 85). When asked to open a new elementary school in South Central Los Angeles, Cordova brought with him a reimagined style and vision that transformed school faculty, families, and community members into leaders.

Using a Critical Participatory Action Researchers (CPAR) methodology, Baxter and Toe (2021) explored the experiences of seven school leaders from three diverse primary schools in Melbourne, Australia, as they experimented with engaging families remotely using social media. These questions guided the study:

- How do school leaders support classroom teachers to engage families in their children's learning via social media?

- How do school leadership structures influence classroom teachers' capacity to engage families in their children's learning via social media?

Baxter and Toe chose the CPAR method for two reasons: its focus on critically examining local practices and the value it places on participatory perspectives and experiences. Using the method, the school leaders engaged educators in reflective discussions about social media.

What Is the Critical Participatory Action Research (CPAR) Method?

The CPAR method is "rooted in the belief that those most impacted by research should take the lead in framing the questions, design, methods, analysis and determining what products and actions might be most useful in effecting change" (Torre, 2009, p. 1).

At one of the schools, educators used those discussions to reassess the use of social media posts to families. They wondered whether families would feel better supported and become more active participants in their children's learning if they shifted their social media posts from merely *informing* families about children's learning (involvement) to *including* families as active participants in their children's learning (engagement). For example, teachers incorporated questions and conversation prompts into their posts that parents could use to talk with their children about what they're learning. By changing the prompts in a social media platform, families experienced a positive shift in understanding about their children's learning, which then led to more reflection about and additional shifts in practice.

These studies suggest that a shift in practices occurs when teachers and school leaders "listen with their ears" to families and embrace practices that value and treat families as partners. Those shifts disrupt traditional mental models that educators embrace and activate new, more dynamic models of family engagement.

Big Story 3: Cultivating and nourishing family partnerships leads to a positive school culture and retention of staff.

Any district leader will tell you that a consistent and growing area of concern is the retention of school staff, particularly of teachers, counselors, and leaders. The studies we've chosen suggest that meaningful family engagement impacts educators' views of their school's culture, their willingness to remain in their jobs, and their overall feelings of well-being.

Educators report a more positive climate and culture.

In their study of Austin Interfaith's decade-long Alliance Schools parent and community organizing effort, Mediratta, Shah, and McAlister (2009) found that, in addition to positive outcomes such as access to new resources, schools highly involved with Austin Interfaith experienced additional outcomes impacting school climate and culture.

- Significant shifts in climate occurred, including increasing the following:
  - teacher-parent trust
  - sense of school community and safety
  - achievement-oriented culture
  - teacher outreach to parents
  - parent influence in school decision-making
  - parent involvement in the school.
- The professional culture improved, specifically on measures related to teacher collegiality, morale, and joint problem-solving.

- Teachers credited Austin Interfaith with a high degree of influence on the quality of school leadership.

- Parents reported greater access to important information, opportunities for communication, and respect from school staff.

- Administrators attributed the strong professional culture to the relational strategies that were introduced by Austin Interfaith and practiced by school staff.

Educators stay at schools where teacher-parent trust is high.

Allensworth, Ponisciak, and Mazzeo, (2009) found that relationships between home and school influenced the retention of teachers. They examined factors associated with high teacher mobility in Chicago Public Schools (CPS), including those teachers' backgrounds, school structure, student characteristics, and workplace conditions, to identify ones that promote retention or trigger departures.

The researchers examined conditions such as school leadership, climate for student learning, and teachers' relationships with their principal, parents, and other teachers. Surveys of teachers and students revealed their thoughts about professional capacity, learning climate, instructional leadership, and parent involvement.

The researchers found that two working conditions account for most of the differences in retention rates: teachers' relationships with parents and teachers' perceptions of students' behavior. Teachers are more likely to stay in schools where they feel that:

- They have influence over school decisions.

- They have the support of principals and cooperative colleagues who help them do their job well.

- They have families that respect and trust them.

Allensworth and her colleagues state:

> *Many (high turnover) schools find it difficult to establish trusting relationships with parents due to high rates of student mobility or cultural differences between teachers and parents. More is expected of teachers in these schools, and it is not surprising that teachers leave these schools at particularly high rates. Yet, we also know that students' behaviors and parental involvement are not completely out of the influence of the school. Schools cannot choose the parents they serve, but they can design their outreach to parents in ways that encourage productive collaboration with teachers, rather than anger and resentment (p. 31).*

Educators report feelings of well-being and professionalism.

In her book, *Natural Allies: Hope and Possibility in Teacher-Family Partnerships* (2019), Soo Hong reveals how partnerships with families positively impact educators' feelings of well-being and satisfaction. Her ethnographic study explored the ways that families and educators worked together to identify the practices and support necessary to create authentic partnerships.

Specifically, Hong examined the motivations and experiences of five urban teachers in Boston and Washington, D. C., who were committed to partnering with and sustaining the cultures of families. Questions that guided the study were:

- What do family-school relationships look like and how do they progress over the school year?

- What motivates teachers to build those relationships?

- How do teachers and parents describe their interactions and relationship?

What Is Portraiture?

Portraiture is a method of social science inquiry recognized for its blending of art and science, capturing the complexity, dynamics, and subtlety of human experience and organizational life. Sara Lawrence-Lightfoot pioneered and used portraiture to document cultures of institutions, life stories of individuals, stages of human development, and essential relationships, processes, and concepts. (From saralawrencelightfoot. com/portraiture1.html)

Hong used *portraiture*, a research method developed by Sara Lawrence-Lightfoot, to conduct her study of the five teachers (1997). Rather than focusing on the "problems" of family-school relationships, Hong explored the "goodness and humanity" of them.

In addition to identifying key practices by teachers to develop trusting and respectful relationships with families, the study found that, across the five narratives, the relationships helped to:

- Combat the isolation of classroom teaching. Engaging with parents provided an important source of collaboration and shared purpose that is often missing in teaching.

- Reinvigorate a professional pathway. The relationships breathed new life into a professional journey that often lacked leadership opportunities and new roles for teachers.

- Offer opportunities for teacher leadership—in some cases, alongside parent leaders.

- Create stronger commitments to and greater success with students through close collaboration with families. Teachers came to see classroom dilemmas as problem-solving opportunities with parents.

- Develop greater collective multicultural awareness. Teachers challenged personal biases and assumptions about families and communities, while offering new insight about themselves as individuals to families.

- Create opportunities to focus on schoolwide practices and school climate. Teachers came to understand the need for continuity of key practices beyond their individual classrooms.

Partnerships between families and educators cultivate positive school climate and culture, help to retain educators, and foster a sense of well-being for everyone in the building. But they may resonate most with those asking, "Where's the beef?", when it comes to the power of partnerships between families and educators.

Big Story 4: Sustaining meaningful family engagement requires certain skills, mindsets, and dispositions.

An exciting trend in the research is a focus on identifying best practices and strategies to build meaningful and trusting partnerships with families, particularly with nondominant families. In their article, *Embracing a New Normal: Toward a More Liberatory Approach to Family Engagement*, Mapp and Bergman (2021) call for practices and strategies that are liberatory (free of dominance), solidarity-driven (in union and fellowship), and equity-focused (fair and just) in order to build trusting partnerships. Several studies we reviewed align with this call for liberatory, solidarity-driven, and equity-focused work. They suggest the following skills, mindsets, and dispositions.

Commit to building trusting relationships with families.

Educators *must* commit to the intentional and ongoing practice of building trust with families. They must also develop the mindsets and dispositions to carry out that trust-building work with families from diverse backgrounds and cultures.

In their study of five school leaders, Osly Flores and Eric Kyere (2020) highlighted that commitment. They focused on five urban school principals, four African American and one White, who encourage social justice practices to engage and empower families and who view family engagement as critical to equitable practice.

Using interviews and external and internal communications with families, Flores and Kyere found that those school leaders embraced the "power of relationships" as a fundamental core belief, stating:

Each participant believed that without a trusting relationship with parents, opportunity to leverage the strength and resources in families may be lost or underutilized. Parent-school involvement thus provides the context for establishing a synergy between the school and the home for the benefit of the child.

For the participants in this study, the idea of human relationship was seen as central to genuine parent engagement. Dr. Thompson states, "I never shied away from difficult kids or difficult parents, [and] difficult communities... human relationships were really important to me" (p. 134).

The educators in this study viewed relationship-building with families as the *fundamental first step* in establishing a positive culture at the school and ensuring student success. They also saw relationship-building as fundamental to their own growth as educators. For example, one principal of an urban elementary school said:

Relationships teach you, relationships grow you, relationships change you, relationships make you better... because of the relationships that we are able to build that, if I have a relationship with a parent, that parent trust(s) me wholeheartedly (p. 135).

Margaret Caspe and M. Elena Lopez's research (2018) focused on librarians, who frequently connect with families, students, and community members, but are too often overlooked.

To determine what librarians should be taught about the importance of meaningful family and community engagement, Caspe and Lopez interviewed 11 educators at top U.S. schools of information and library sciences. They asked questions about the knowledge, skills, and dispositions new librarians should have, to work successfully with families and communities. They also asked questions about current training for librarians and the extent to which their education covered family and community engagement topics. The educators were also asked to reflect on the best teaching methods, or pedagogy, to discuss family and community engagement topics with future librarians.

The researchers' bottom line: Help librarians build relationships with families and communities. Their study suggested the following ways to do that. Librarians should:

- Move beyond simply knowing their patrons to develop the cultural competence to work closely with them.

- Listen to families and community members and work to understand their perspectives.

- Develop skills such as being flexible, identifying and solving problems, and, above all, communicating strongly and transparently.

- Forge relationships with community organizations. When librarians know who is doing what work in their communities, they can reach out and co-create programming.

In sum, Caspe and Lopez noted that when strong and trusting relationships are developed, partnerships are most successful.

Resist and reject deficit thinking about families and communities.

Given the influence of our learned biases and the "smog of prejudice" (Tatum, 2017) that we breathe every day, it's important to resist and reject deficit thinking about families and communities, and to see them through an asset-based lens.

Flores and Kyere (2020) identified three resistance practices that school leaders in their study use to push against deficit thinking at external and personal levels.

1. **The school leaders reframe challenges as opportunities.** When faced with low turnout at evening parent council events, one leader, Dr. Thompson, took advantage of the large numbers of families that showed up at the school each morning to drop off their children. Seeing that as an opportunity to connect with families, rather than judging them for their inability to attend evening events, Dr. Thompson created "mocha Mondays," a morning space where families could eat and engage in conversations about school.

2. **The school leaders persevere when others want to quit.** When their staff becomes discouraged with family engagement activities or time-consuming efforts that do not immediately yield expected results, these leaders remain persistent and remind staff of the power of family engagement.

3. **The school leaders confront themselves to avoid crossing the border into deficit thinking.** The study reveals how leaders engage in critical self-reflection to challenge their own biases when they arise. The authors describe the process of one school leader to check and resist deficit-thinking about her families.

When asked what has been a challenge in her work towards equity, Dr. Grant took a long, deep sigh and said, "The first challenge I have every day is I challenge my own white privilege. To be honest with you, 'cause I get upset many times with how parents show up and how they show up with their children."

> *Although Dr. Grant is a black female, she acknowledges that her position as principal within the institution of education has influenced her enculturation of elements of white privilege in her practice.... According to Dr. Grant, she tries to check her deficit thinking at "the door and see how I still can be a support to that parent" and "begin [to] see how I can minister to the needs of my parents to get them on the road to whatever self-actualization that there is* (p. 137).

Those three practices by school leaders—to reframe challenges as opportunities, to preserve when others want to quit, and to confront themselves to avoid crossing the border into deficit thinking—provide powerful advice to educators who want to commit to liberatory and equitable partnerships with all families.

Another practice identified in the research was the importance of getting to know families as individuals and not just as members of groups. The McKnight et al. study (2017) discussed earlier in this chapter revealed how relational home visits created a space for *individuation*— or the process of families and educators experiencing each other as unique individuals—to happen, rather than stereotypes. One educator stated:

> *These home visits really give me insight into families and the community as individual people with their own lives and issues. It just breaks apart a stereotype, because if you have those counterexamples, the stereotypes can no longer exist.* (p. 27)

Communicate with families by listening to them and truly caring about them.

We hear all the time that communication between educators and families should be "two-way." What does that mean? What does two-way communication look like in practice? What dispositions do educators have to hold to engage in it with families? On page 100, we offer high-impact strategies and practices for ensuring two-way communications with families. Here, we "get under the hood" and describe the dispositions and mindsets required to implement those strategies and practices with fidelity. What do we need to know about the purposes and meaning of communications with families for them to be successful? In what ways do we need to "show up" for them?

In *Natural Allies* (2019), Soo Hong tells us the rich and textured stories of five urban teachers—Ilene Carver, Megan Lucas, Cinthia Colón, Annie Shaw, and Julia Finkelstein—and how they build and navigate partnerships with diverse families. Those stories elevate the genuine care, thoughtfulness, and commitment to listening to all students' families. Ilene Carver describes how she communicates with families:

> *My first interaction and every subsequent conversation with a parent reflects a deep sense of caring. I think it's much easier to say that we want these conversations to be positive, and we certainly don't want them to be negative. But what's always on my mind is, "Do they know that they are important to me? Do they get a sense that I care about their child?" Part of that comes from a willingness to listen to parents, to ask them questions, invite them to support me and give me feedback on what I'm doing. But it's also reflected in my desire to keep that conversation going and to continue to make them feel that they are important (p. 172).*

It's clear that Ilene makes the communication of *care*, rather than policies and procedures or rules and regulations, her top priority. Her goal in early communications with families is to let them know their importance and the importance of their child, and her care comes through in her disposition and commitment to *listen* to families.

Families respond positively to a deeply caring stance, which is clear in these words of a parent of one of Ms. Colón's students:

> *At this point, when I hear from Ms. Colón, I feel completely at ease. Over all the times we have talked in person or on the phone or by text, we now have a history of working together. I don't feel threatened or nervous when I hear from her, and I know that whatever we do talk about, it's going to be improving the situation for Trey; I have no doubt about that (p. 172).*

NAFSCE's Family Engagement Core Competencies

The National Association for Family, School, and Community Engagement (NAFSCE) has been working in collaboration with higher education leaders, parent leadership organizations, educators, and state education agencies to develop a set of core competencies for practitioners. Go here for a chart listing those competencies: https://nafsce.org/page/CoreCompetencies.

The Hong study provides clear markers for developing two-way communication with families. Far too often, traditional communication is compliance-driven and distant, with no room for sharing stories and knowledge—the very ingredients needed to build trust. The study paves the way for effective communication with families by showcasing the way the five teachers listened to and truly cared for families. Hong states:

When considering parent-teacher communications, we traditionally focus on what teachers communicate to parents. This is usually the focus of parent-teacher conferences and the stance in school events designed for families. What this implies to parents and caregivers is that the most useful knowledge about a child's education originates at the school, but in the case of all five teachers in this study, they place a high premium on listening to parents as well…These teachers, thus, establish parent-teacher communications as a two-way endeavor (p. 172).

Big Story 5: Supporting effective family engagement requires resources, leadership, and infrastructure.

Without the proper training to work in solidarity with families, even the most seasoned educators can struggle. It's simply not enough to have a strong desire and good intentions. In fact, without training, educators can develop negative mindsets about family engagement when things don't go as planned (Hong, 2011).

In her book, *The Essential Conversation: What Parents and Teachers Can Learn From Each Other*, Sara Lawrence-Lightfoot explores the parent-teacher conference, a signature event held at most schools. The teachers she interviewed for the book admit that they often fear conversations with families because they do not know how to lead them. Their professional training—both pre-service and in-service—did not adequately prepare them to engage meaningfully and effectively with families. As a result, many felt vulnerable when interacting with families.

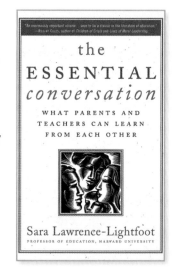

Another study revealing the need for training in and support for family engagement was conducted by Barbour, Eisenstadt, Goodall, Jelley, and Sylva (2018), and examined the effects of five early intervention programs run by organizations in the UK designed to help low-income families strengthen the home learning environment. This study, conducted in collaboration with the Parental Engagement Fund (PEF), compared five interventions to change parents' home learning practices during their children's early years. Its goals were to address inequality in children's early learning and develop effective family engagement practice.

The study ushered in a new model for identifying effective family engagement practices by developing the capacity of the organizations to design, deliver, and evaluate their own interventions.

The participating organizations established the following goals:

- Increase families' participation in engagement activities.
- Increase evidence of impact on parents' interaction with their children, including the home learning environment.
- Increase evidence of program impact on children's learning outcomes.
- Develop the organizations' capacity for self-evaluation.
- Improve the quality of evidence of impact using a rigorous framework.
- Leverage support and resources for future growth.

PEF provided three forms of support:

1. Funding to help each organization deliver its program to a target group within the trial period.

2. A "critical friend" in the form of a team from Oxford's Department of Education to coach each group in the evaluation process. This included identifying evidence on implementation and impact, developing a theory of change to show the pathway of effects on children, and selecting an evaluation model. Further coaching covered carrying out their trials, collecting data, doing analysis, and considering results.

3. Monthly catch-ups to develop strategies for delivery and creating a network to share ideas and results. PEF also assisted with publicity and communication and the connected groups to potential funders and markets.

A total of 1,329 families (parent-child pairs) took part in the PEF programs. Findings were broken into four categories, and two of them pinpointed the need for and benefits of practitioner support and training:

1. **What helps early childhood practitioners to engage families?**

   Support from senior management: Providing cover and time for preparation was key to success, practitioners said.

   Positive attitudes toward parents: A common benchmark for change is realizing that all parents want the best for their children. Teachers described how much the training helped them to better understand parents. They also remarked on the value of supporting parents in helping their children's learning and settling into school.

   Realizing the benefits to staff: Early childhood practitioners noted changes in their practice, in their understanding of the value of parents' engagement, and in their skills to support that engagement. To staff, the projects were valuable professional development that built capacity across their setting.

2. What are the pros and cons of various models of delivery?

Among the projects, there were two approaches: training practitioners/teachers and direct delivery of services to families. Training the practitioner appears to leave a legacy in the early childhood setting, where improved capacity would lead to sustained use of the practices. Practitioners said they greatly appreciated the training and planned to continue using what they learned.

Practitioners in the study commented on how the experience helped them gain greater understanding of the means and value of engaging parents. This, in turn, strengthened their confidence and capacity to support that engagement. Practitioners also appreciated the projects as an effective form of continuing professional development.

Big Story 4 underscores the fact that educators must have the opportunity, through training, practice, and support, to develop the skills to achieve partnerships with families, to develop positive and asset-based mindsets about *all* families, and to acquire the spirit and emotional center to ground their family engagement practice. Educators cannot be expected "go forth and develop" partnerships with families on their own. Systems and structures must support them.

Conclusion

Our reasons for writing this book were to add to what we know about the impact of family engagement on student outcomes, but also to reveal the benefits of family engagement to the adults who come together to support students. This chapter focused on the benefits to one group of adults—educators—and our review of the studies found there are many "wins" for them.

Partnerships with families allow educators to shift to fresh, asset-based ways of thinking about the role of families and imagine new ways to partner with them. Educators find the school environment and their practice more enjoyable, fulfilling, and effective because of their partnerships with families. But to build the skills, mindsets, and dispositions necessary for effective family engagement, educators need training and ongoing guidance, bolstered by systems and structures that support that work.

CHAPTER 3

FAMILY ENGAGEMENT AND FAMILIES
Impact and Benefits

April Ybarra, a parent at Oak Ridge Elementary School in Sacramento, California, recounts her experience with home visits:

"Before the Parent/Teacher Home Visits Project, I was very close-minded about the school, very negative. When I was a student at Oak Ridge, the teachers there were unsupportive of my needs and other students'. So, when my kids started their education at Oak Ridge, I already had put up a barrier between me and the school because I wanted to protect my children. The principal and assistant principal tried to build a relationship with me, even though I was always negative toward them and stand-offish. No way would I agree to a home visit from a teacher. But then my daughter started to struggle, and they took that as an opportunity to woo me into doing the first visit.

I'll never forget that. On the visit, the teacher asked me, 'What are your hopes and dreams for your child?' And I realized that anybody who comes into my home, in a nonjudgmental way, and asks me that question must really care. So, I just let that barrier drop. Anything I can do to help, support, and be a part of the school community, I now do.

The home visit has given parents like me a voice. I feel a lot more confident about voicing what I feel is best for my child's education, and I also feel when I do raise my voice I'm actually heard, and my child's educational needs will be addressed.

Both my children are reading much better. They are English language learners, and when they started school, they didn't speak any English. By the end of kindergarten, my oldest still didn't know much English, and that was scary for me. After our first home visit, when she was in first grade, she got the help she needed, and she was reading at grade level by the end of the year. And that went for other children, not just my daughter.

One of the biggest supports is combining the home visits with Academic Parent Teacher Teams because a lot of parents like me don't know how to help their children with subjects they are struggling in.

The Parent/Teacher Home Visits Project has definitely helped me to build a relationship with the school, and it's grown into a community thing. It's not just about building relationships between the teacher and home, but also building relationships among parents in the community, and that's pretty cool.

I think the project helps teachers better understand parents and our busy lives. And for us parents, we see there are teachers who really do care about the education of our children, and that they are not there just to collect a paycheck, which is what I used to believe. Now I know it's not like that."

This chapter focuses on the "family" in family engagement for student success, showcasing studies that demonstrate how family engagement practices, initiatives, and frameworks are understood and experienced by parents and other caregivers. The studies prove that family engagement—or lack thereof—impacts how students' family members, including but not limited to their parents, siblings, and extended family members, understand their role in their children's education and their ability to have an impact on it. Thus, it is essential to consider how families themselves experience family engagement practices.

- In what ways does a family's sense of self-efficacy and personal development change depending on its relationships with those in the school?

- From the family's perspective, what elements are essential to develop strong relationships with teachers?

- What does the research tell us about the barriers to engagement that families experience?

We answer those questions and others by extrapolating information from the 16 studies that speak to the impact of family engagement on families. Simply put, this chapter centers families' experiences.

These studies focus on how families experience engagement. What they all have in common is that they illustrate, to varying degrees, how families benefit from family engagement practices. Thus, we have divided this conversation into five big stories:

1. Practicing family engagement strengthens families' sense of self-efficacy.

2. Investing in family engagement practices develops families' leadership capabilities.

3. Facing barriers prevents families from engaging with their children's education.

4. Recognizing families' daily lives and circumstances influences the nature of their engagement.

5. Communicating clearly, openly, and regularly is essential for strong family-school partnerships and information sharing.

When taken together, these studies offer insight into the realities, possibilities, and promises of family engagement, particularly for students' families.

Big Story 1: Practicing family engagement strengthens families' sense of self-efficacy.

Family engagement practices strengthen families' sense of self-efficacy, or the belief that they can impact their children's education. In short, it has a transformative effect on families: When families believe they have a role in their children's education, they become more actively engaged. Clear and open communication between families and educators allows families to understand the importance of their role in their children's education. Similarly, connecting families to each other and developing family networks are key to developing their sense of self-efficacy. It's important to create opportunities for families to meet and build connections to create trusting relationships.

Establish strong, trusting relationships with families.

In their study of Achievement for All, a program to improve outcomes for children with special educational needs and disabilities in the United Kingdom, Humphrey and Squires (2011) noted the dramatic effects of "Structured Conversations about Learning" between teachers and parents. (This study is covered in more detail in Chapters 1 and 2.) Not only did student achievement, self-confidence, and motivation improve, but exchanges of valuable information between parents and teachers greatly increased. Parents gained new insights into their children, allowing them to enrich and effectively encourage their learning and development. In other words, parents' sense of self-efficacy in supporting their children's education increased.

This story illustrates the point well:

Both his parents and teacher described Elliot as an "outdoor child." If he was in a classroom for too long, he became frustrated and started to struggle with his writing. He also had some difficulties in social relationships and self-esteem. After the Structured Conversations

with Elliot's parents, his teacher saw considerable improvements in his confidence and academic progress. Although Elliot's mother initially said she just wanted her child to be happy, the teacher challenged her by saying that Elliot could achieve in school. Elliot's teacher also reported that he was aware that his mother and teacher had been talking and working together.

In her account of the Structured Conversations, Elliot's mother said that the school is "always quite eager to hear what I have to say or if I have any ideas to help them. So, yeah, they are very good like that. We help each other on the way. Like I say, they do listen to a lot, they are quite happy to take on board everything that I am saying because it sort of makes their job that little bit easier as well." The teacher reported that Elliot's mindset shifted to thinking he was capable of being an achiever, and consequently his writing scores improved significantly (Humphrey and Squires, 2011, p. 99).

Empower families by developing family networks.

Rangel, Shoji, and Gamoran's (2020) study examined what factors, beyond just "knowing" other parents, lead to building high quality networks of mutual support. The parents in their study described the type of interactions that can foster deeper relationships, which included:

- determining the trustworthiness of other parents
- expressing care and respect for one another
- reciprocity, or doing things for one another

This study revealed that deeper relationships were forged through intensive interactions that allowed parents to determine trustworthiness, express care and respect for one another, and exchange favors. The authors note that, within a typical school community, the casual nature of encounters with other families does not create relationships that parents consider trusting and meaningful. Even in school gatherings that bring families together, the opportunities for parents to talk with each other are brief and infrequent. The value of a network to families is based on the level of exchange of useful interactions and resources.

Big Story 2: Investing in family engagement practices develops families' leadership capabilities.

In addition to developing their sense of self-efficacy, family engagement practices also transform families' leadership skills. In other words, when given the opportunity to be equal partners with their children's educators, family members experience personal, empowering transformations.

Invest in developing family leadership.

Geller and colleagues (2019) highlight the importance of leadership development in their evaluation of seven parent leadership initiatives (PLIs) from across the United States. In their study, they found that investment in family strengthening and healing-centered engagement led to transformational outcomes for parent leaders, and their families and communities. Parent leaders moved from seeing themselves as "just a parent," a "victim," or a "worrier," to "change agents," "role models," and the "go-to people" in their families and community.

Additionally, Geller and colleagues noted that the PLIs saw their efforts as a tool for making positive social change by cultivating the self-worth, agency, and dignity of parent leaders. They also identified five practices that led to these profound and transformative impacts:

1. Meeting parents' individual needs and goals through a commitment to fostering families' well-being and building on their strengths.

2. Creating a community that feels like a family—one that is welcoming, supportive, and free of judgment and stigma, and that appreciates, validates, and affirms their efforts.

3. Developing solidarity across racial, economic, and cultural differences by creating a sense of positive identity and pride in one's culture and practicing consciousness-raising about inequities in society.

4. Empowering parents through skill- and knowledge-building, and then using that information to interact directly with community leaders.

5. Creating stable and ongoing support and serving as a "safe haven" where parents are always welcomed back.

What parents say about themselves after attending leadership training

- Developed deep and supportive social connections resembling a "second family."

- Discovered their own worth and voice, and a sense of power to make change.

- Stopped blaming themselves for their struggles and came to understand that policies and systems can create barriers to opportunity and advancement.

- Learned to understand and appreciate differences across race, ethnicity, education, language, religion, sexual orientation, gender identity, and country of origin, and to create unity and agreement within a diverse group.

- Grew more dedicated to taking action in their community, which deepened as their sense of agency and commitment to each other grew.

- Created a more positive sense of possibility for themselves and their community.

- Were seen with new respect by their children and families, who were inspired to take action themselves.

(Geller et al., 2019. *The Ripple Effect in Action*.)

Similarly, in her book *A Cord of Three Strands: A New Approach to Parent Engagement in Schools*, Hong (2011) provides an in-depth account and analysis of the work of the Palenque LSNA. Central to the work of Palenque LSNA is its Parent Mentor Program, which has trained over 1,300 parents to work in classrooms with teachers and to support student learning and development. Using a model for leadership development, the Parent Mentor Program serves as an initial step not only for parent participation in schools, but also for long-term engagement as parent leaders.

Based on her observations, Hong designed a framework called *the ecology of parent engagement*. This three-part ecological model considers the multiple contexts, interactions, and experiences that shape parent engagement:

1. **Parent engagement as induction:** developing engagement and participation opportunities that are designed to introduce parents to school environments and practices. These strategies acknowledge the personal and institutional barriers that parents may face in becoming involved in schools as well as the linguistic and cultural experiences that make them seemingly "hard to reach."

2. **Parent engagement as integration:** highlighting the ways engagement strategies can connect parents to other individuals in the school. These strategies emphasize the role that relationships—with other parents, families, students, and school staff—play in sustaining parent involvement over time.

3. **Parent engagement as investment:** envisioning parent engagement in ways that build parents as leaders and active decision-makers within schools. Viewing parents as individuals with valuable skills, resources, and assets, these strategies move parents from serving as passive participants to active contributors in schools.

Both the Geller and colleagues and Hong studies show that transformational change not only alters parents' sense of identity and purpose, but also shifts power relationships so that parents can use their newfound confidence to speak out and demand better opportunities for their children and families.

Use community-organizing strategies to develop family leaders.

When families are engaged on a personal and collaborative level, they develop into leaders who work towards educational equity and social justice (Warren et al., 2015). As the Geller et al. study found, community organizing strategies can help individual parents develop their leadership skills and capacities. In their study of the Northwest Bronx Community and Clergy Coalition, Warren and colleagues (2015) found that parents who were involved in community organizing experienced a transformational change from private citizens to public actors and change agents. In other words, parents who were involved in community organizing developed the skills, confidence, and sense of self-efficacy to demand social change for the sake of their children. Furthermore, Warren and colleagues identified six interrelated processes through which community organizing empowers parents to undergo this transformation. These include:

What Does the Ecology of Parent Engagement Look Like in Practice?

"From the beginning, we always had this concept of parent-teacher mentoring—the teacher mentoring the parent, but the parent was also helping the teacher understand about the culture of the community."

—Nancy Aardema, former LSNA Executive Director

- listening
- building parent community
- mentoring
- encouraging risk-taking
- learning through action
- linking the personal and the political

Through engaging parents in these processes and scaffolding leadership responsibilities, community organizers help parents develop into leaders who work towards sustainable, systemic change in their schools and communities (Warren et al., 2015).

Big Story 3: Facing barriers prevents families from engaging with their children's education.

Families face challenges, or barriers, to engaging with their children's education. Recent research has borne out that it is essential to identify and address those barriers to improve our family engagement practices. In much of this research, scholars and practitioners have noted that there are certain elements that prevent the development of trusting relationships between families and schools. Those barriers include lack of time (e.g., overworked teachers without enough time to communicate with parents or parents juggling multiple jobs), distrust between parents and teachers, language barriers, and misinformation or miscommunication between parents and teachers.

Whether it involves parents' struggling to adapt their work schedules to attend school events, such as open houses or parent-teacher conferences, or teachers' assuming parents are unable to help their children with their homework, research shows that many assumptions impact how families and schools work with each other. Here are some strategies to improve family-school partnerships.

How Do We Define "Parent and Family Engagement"?

As noted in the introduction, the definition for parent and family engagement has changed throughout the years to be more inclusive of various family structures. Yet there is often still confusion about what we mean when we talk about parent engagement. For example, in their study, Baker and colleagues defined it as intentional efforts by the school to recognize and respond to parents' voices and to help school staff to better understand how to address barriers that parents have identified" (Baker et al., 2016, p. 163).

Identify barriers to family engagement.

There are benefits in recognizing families' challenges to engagement. For example, Baker and colleagues (2016) sought to identify challenges with hopes of increasing parent engagement.

Based on interviews with parents and school staff, the researchers found that parents' barriers to engagement included lack of childcare, responsibilities such as feeding the family before school events, and work constraints (Baker et al., 2016). The study also underlined the importance of communication, with parents noting the lack of, quality of, and clarity of communication as barriers to engaging with their children's schools.

In addition to those barriers, more recent studies are also identifying difficulties previously unknown to educators. For example, in her study of how undocumented Latinx parents are engaged in their children's higher education aspirations,

Cuevas (2019) illustrates how an undocumented immigration status impacts parents' engagement in their children's education.

Because undocumented immigrants do not have legal permanent residency or U.S. citizenship, they live with the daily fear that they can be asked for proof of residency and, upon failing to provide it, could be detained, deported, and separated from their families. In her study, Cuevas illustrated how undocumented parents risked deportation and unemployment during everyday tasks such as driving their children to school activities. It's clear that undocumented immigration status is an additional barrier educators must consider (2019).

Be on alert for misinformed assumptions about families and schools.

Other barriers to family-school partnerships are the assumptions that families and educators make about each other. Lack of sustained communication prevents families and schools from developing strong relationships (Baker et al., 2016), which is at the root of misinformed assumptions. For instance, parents may assume that they only need to be in touch with teachers when their children are not doing well in school. At the same time, teachers may assume that parents who do not attend school events do not care about their children's education. Both outlooks, or assumptions, are due to the lack of trusting relationships between parents and teachers.

That lack of trusting relationships and, consequently, lack of empathy are at the root of Sara Lawrence-Lightfoot's book, *The Essential Conversation: What Parents and Teachers Can Learn From Each Other* (2003). In this in-depth, qualitative study, Lawrence-Lightfoot took a close look at the interactions that happen during the parent-teacher conference. She found that both parties are often unprepared, nervous, and anxious during conferences. Much like the parents in Baker et al.'s study who reported feeling intimidated by school personnel and believed it to be a barrier to their relationships with teachers, Lawrence-Lightfoot observed that parents were often reserved and defensive (2003).

Furthermore, she notes that parents and teachers tend to enter conferences with their own "autobiographical and psychological scripts." If parents have only had negative interactions with teachers in the past, they are going to be defensive. Subconsciously, then, they may create negative assumptions about teachers' intentions toward their children. Lawrence-Lightfoot notes that those scripts, or "ghosts," if left unexamined, can lead to barriers during parent-teacher conferences.

Challenges Faced by Undocumented Immigrant Families

Undocumented immigrants face challenges such as work instability, workplace discrimination, and limited or no access to social services such as healthcare and rent control. Additionally, undocumented parents often must consider the possibility of deportation as they navigate everyday life.

Make family engagement a systemic value.

A final barrier noted in the studies is that schools do not value parents as equal partners in students' education. In essence, this barrier is an accumulation and consequence of all the barriers described thus far: When there is no clear communication between families and schools (Baker et al., 2016; Lawrence-Lightfoot, 2003) or understanding of families' needs (such as language translation, childcare, and alternate scheduling), families do not feel respected by school staff. This, then, prevents trusting relationships from developing.

In her research, Ishimaru (2019) found that family engagement needs to be embedded in all aspects of school and other educational entities, such as after-school programs and non-profit organizations. To help families feel like they belong in the school and see themselves as essential partners with educators, family engagement efforts need to be systemwide and not just individual efforts. (Ishimaru, 2019). For example, schoolwide decisions must be in collaboration with families and students, allowing them to have a say in school policy changes. Simply put, family engagement needs to be systemic for it to become a core value.

Big Story 4: Recognizing families' daily lives and circumstances influences the nature of their engagement.

Research has shown again and again that families' abilities to engage in their children's education are influenced by a variety of factors and circumstances, such as race, ethnicity, class, gender, socioeconomic status, and immigrant generation (when the family migrated to the United States). Family engagement does not occur in a vacuum. This research illustrates and highlights the importance of considering how families' lives may impact their engagement with their children's schools.

Parents are more likely to engage when they feel welcomed (Hoover-Dempsey et al., 2005; Jensen & Minke, 2017). Parents are motivated by their beliefs about their responsibilities for their child's education and whether their actions have a positive influence on outcomes (Hoover-Dempsey et al., 2005; Jensen & Minke, 2017). Thus, when educators understand the life contexts of families, they can intentionally make families feel welcomed in family-school partnerships.

Be sensitive to the timing of family engagement.

The earlier family-school relationships develop, the better the outcomes for students. This point is at the core of Momoko Hayakawa and colleagues' (2013) longitudinal study of Chicago Center Child-Parent program (CPC). As described in Chapter 1, the authors found that early parent involvement directly influenced kindergarten achievement, which in turn influenced first grade student motivation. Highly motivated children then encouraged parents to continue involvement, creating a positive cyclical process.

Modify family engagement as students move up the grades.

Just as it is important to consider when family engagement begins, it is equally important to understand its dynamic and changing nature. Research has also demonstrated that the nature of family engagement changes as students progress through their K–12 education.

For example, in their literature review of parent engagement research at the secondary level, Jensen and Minke (2017) found that parent engagement maintains a positive relationship with academic achievement through high school. Yet, these engagement behaviors are different from those traditionally performed at the elementary level: Significant behaviors include those that are more subtle and less direct than school-centric involvement, focusing instead on academic socialization.

Other important factors include parents' supporting students' self-autonomy and independence, parental monitoring, and the conditions of the home environment. Higher parent engagement rates are also positively associated with increased high school graduation rates, and they trend with lower rates of adolescent anxiety, depression, and aggressive behaviors.

What Is "Academic Socialization"?

Academic socialization refers to the "communication-based behaviors from parents that convey the importance of education, their aspirations for the adolescent, and plans for the future" (Jensen & Minke, 2017, p. 171). Examples include parents asking children about their favorite part of the school day or conversations about potential careers.

Consider families' backgrounds in family engagement practices.

Research that focuses on marginalized populations, such as families of color, immigrant families, and low-income families, has called for engagement and partnership opportunities that are more culture-specific, culturally relevant, or culturally sustaining. For example, in her study of undocumented Latinx parents, Cuevas (2019) notes that parents' undocumented immigration status leads them to engage in "concerted *sacrificios*." (See below.)

Because they were undocumented immigrants, the parents in her study faced the risk of deportation and family separation, had constrained access to social services, and were exposed to undesirable work conditions, among other barriers (Cuevas, 2019). Cuevas notes that it is essential to consider this context when engaging and partnering with families.

Similarly, in their study of Puerto Rican fathers in New York State, Quiñones and Kiyama (2014) underline the importance of considering parents' intersecting racial, ethnic, and gender identities. When asked about their relationships with their children's schools, the fathers critiqued the racial/ethnic tensions and racism within home-school-community relations. Fathers reported feeling invisible and discriminated against due to their race/ethnicity and language preferences for Spanish.

Furthermore, both the Cuevas and Quiñones and Kiyama studies note that the parent participants (undocumented Latinx parents and Puerto Rican fathers) were engaged in behaviors like those of middle-class parents. These behaviors included actively monitoring their children's grades and enrolling them in different extracurricular activities. In the case of the Quiñones and Kiyama study, the Puerto Rican fathers "were intentionally playing 'the game' not just because someone told them they should be involved, but because they understood that in order to progress, they had to play by the rules of the middle class, while at the same time critiquing it and their place in it" (p. 169).

What Are "Concerted *Sacrificios*"?

Cuevas defines "concerted *sacrificios*" as the "conscious decisions and investments undocumented Latinx parents make to support their children's educational attainment, which comes at a very high personal cost due to the sociopolitical context they face as undocumented immigrants" (Cuevas, 2019, p. 475).

The undocumented Latinx parents in the Cuevas study, on the other hand, intentionally engaged in such behaviors to support their children's post-secondary aspirations. Factors such as a concern about one's immigration status or challenges participating in a school system that doesn't recognize one's background (e.g., cultural, racial, linguistic) shape how families understand their roles and involvement with their child's education.

Big Story 5: Communicating clearly, openly, and regularly is essential for strong family-school partnerships and information sharing.

The importance of clear, open, and ongoing communication between families and schools is another established theme in family engagement research. As discussed earlier, parents often identify lack of, quality of, and clarity of communication as barriers to engagement. For example, the parents in the study by Baker and colleagues noted that the poor communication made it seem to families that the schools were not family-friendly. The problems associated with communication did not allow parents to form strong relationships with the school staff (Baker et al., 2016). Consequently, the researchers conclude communication needs to be clear, consistent, and linked to learning. Furthermore, schools must open the lines of communication with parents and create opportunities for engagement. In other words, they must communicate with families and invite them to engage in their children's education and partner to ensure their success (Barbour et al., 2018; Baker et al., 2016).

Establish strong communication with families to share important information.

In their nationwide study of parents and teachers, Learning Heroes (2018) found a disconnect between parents' perceptions of their children's academic proficiency and the reality of their performance. The study found that parents were often overconfident about their children's performance.

> Just as most parents think their child is at or above grade level academically, survey findings suggest most parents think their child is happy in school and do not describe their child as "stressed" (p. 8).

Not only might this confidence indicate that some parents do not have the full picture of their children's social-emotional health, but it may also convince them that they don't need to be more involved in school than they already are. As mentioned in the previous chapter, parents need to be given information and resources to help them appropriately interpret and understand their children's educational records (e.g., report cards, test results).

Similarly, Learning Heroes noted that teachers need to be trained on how to effectively communicate with parents: many teachers do not have formal training on how to handle difficult conversations with parents, nor do they have adequate administrative support. The authors conclude by noting that:

> Providing parents and teachers with the same… clear, decipherable information can lead to more meaningful teacher-parent discussions, which will help parents to be more engaged and better prepared to support their child at home. It can provide a starting place for building deeper teacher-parent partnerships on behalf of all children (p. 24).

Use technology to improve family engagement practices.

Studies have also focused on best practices to help families and schools share information with each other using technology; technology can improve communication lines between families and schools. For example, social media platforms offer schools new opportunities to enhance communication with families. Digital platforms allow teachers to upload instructional materials (such as photos, video/audio footage, and annotated work samples), with which students, families, and teachers can interact (Baxter & Toe, 2021).

Nevertheless, social media posts also have the potential to confuse and mislead parents when they are rife with educational jargon. If teachers' expectations are not clear when using these tools, families may feel overwhelmed; if families have no access to technology, they may feel even more isolated. To be effective, using technology and social media to partner with families needs to be a sustained practice that occurs throughout the entire school year, rather than "random acts" that are determined by the school (Baxter & Toe, 2021).

For example, in their study of three culturally diverse Australian primary schools, Baxter and Toe (2021) found that constant communication via social media gives families a bigger role in their children's education. As one school learning leader shared with the researchers, after using Flexibuzz School, a social media platform to share learning practices with families:

> When we looked at the first cycle of parent data, the parents reported, "We know what is happening at school." Within the second cycle of data, though, parents were saying, "We know what is happening at school, and we talk about it with our children."

The use of the social media platform changed the nature of communication between families and schools and how families used the information they learned. Studies have also noted that texting interventions are cost-effective engagement strategies (Angrist, 2020; Kraft & Rogers, 2015). Kraft and Rogers (2015) examined weekly, one-sentence, individualized messages from teachers to parents of high school students attending a summer credit recovery program in a large urban school district in the northeastern United States. The aim of the intervention was to increase "parents' efforts and effectiveness at supporting their child's success in school" (pp. 49–50).

The researchers found that messages decreased the percentage of students who failed to earn course credit by 41 percent, primarily by preventing dropouts from the program. Through its success in improving student attendance and passing rates, this intervention highlights the potential to increase parent involvement in their children's education through policy initiatives. Kraft and Rogers recommend designing policies that set specific, achievable expectations for teachers in systems that allow for efficient, effective communication with families, and their study provides evidence that these conditions are not only possible, but impactful.

Similarly, Angrist and colleagues (2020) found that low-cost, low-technology interventions can support communication between families and schools. Conducted in summer 2020 during the COVID-19 pandemic, their study evaluated a rapid randomized trial of two low-technology interventions to substitute in-person schooling in Botswana. The program utilized text messages and direct phone calls to mitigate learning loss and to empower parents of primary school students to engage in their children's education. The researchers found that the low-cost interventions greatly reduced innumeracy (the inability to understand math) and boosted parent engagement. In addition, 98 percent of households wanted to continue the program after the first four weeks.

Make family-school communication ongoing and transparent, especially in troubling times.

Just as the Angrist and colleagues (2020) study illustrated, the COVID-19 pandemic further emphasized the importance of clear and ongoing communication between families and schools. TalkingPoints published a report in June 2021—"Family Engagement, COVID-19, and Distance Learning: Data & Insights from the Field"—to better understand the impact of distance learning on families and educators supporting students in the early days of the pandemic. In June 2021, the nonprofit wanted to examine how these results had changed after an entire year of distance learning, and how family-teacher communication through its platform impacted learning experiences.

The survey found that frequent teacher-family communication during this period positively impacted student learning and well-being. This was especially true for students from non-English speaking families; the online communications were in families' primary language (TalkingPoints, 2021). Additionally, the survey also found that the nature of the communication was essential: when conversations between families and teachers discussed personal student and family matters that may have been impeding student learning or gave insight into particular student needs, teachers felt better prepared to support their students.

The TalkingPoints survey also found that while families felt more connected to their students' teachers than before, there was a disconnect between what parents and teachers were sharing and what each group wanted and needed to know from the other. In other words, there was a mismatch or miscommunication about what the priorities should be once students returned to the classroom:

- Families' priorities were assistance with their children's transition back to the classroom and new grade levels, maintaining communication with teachers, and COVID-19 safety protocols.
- Teachers' priorities, on the other hand, revolved around student learning loss, student socioemotional well-being, and re-engaging students in the physical classroom (TalkingPoints, 2021).

While those priorities are similar, especially when it comes to centering student experiences and well-being upon returning to the classroom, the TalkingPoints report cautioned that families and teachers should communicate to ensure that their priorities are aligned. As educators consider how to recover from the COVID-19 pandemic, or other future disruptions, family-teacher communication and relationships should be a priority.

Furthermore, communication between both parties should center on a mutual understanding of priorities: What do parents and teachers expect from each other as students transition back to the classroom (TalkingPoints, 2021)?

Conclusion

Family engagement practices should not only center on students' needs, but also on families' needs. After all, families are 50 percent of the family-school partnership equation. The research illustrates the power of family engagement in developing families' sense of self-efficacy and leadership skills. These are the wins for families. As such, it is essential for educators to consider each family's life circumstances and how those circumstances may create barriers to or opportunities for engagement. The research discussed in this chapter highlights the importance of communication between families and educators. Families want to remain informed about what is happening in their children's education—and when they are well-informed by a responsive school staff, they are in a better position to effect positive change for their child, their child's teacher, the school, and the community.

CHAPTER 4

FAMILY ENGAGEMENT AND SCHOOLS, DISTRICTS, AND COMMUNITIES

Impact and Benefits

Coliseum College Prep Academy (CCPA), which serves grades six to 12, was created by a community-based design process in Oakland, California. It opened in 2006 after a team of parents, students, staff, and community members gave extensive input during the research and planning process. The result is a community school with a deep commitment to collaborating with families and a tightly integrated web of supports and services to benefit those families. CCPA serves about 500 students, 96 percent of whom are low income, and about half of whom are multilingual learners. Despite those challenges, in 2018, 95 percent were college- and career-ready.

The original vision statement, written by parents and teachers, imagined a school where families would be welcomed and supported, with staff members who speak both Spanish and English, as well as a dedicated space for parents to gather and learn together. It's not unusual for parents to drop into classrooms to observe instruction, and for teachers to rely on parents to maintain the school's rigorous schedule (the school day typically ends at 5 PM) and discipline policies and practices that were co-designed with families.

CCPA builds community by hosting potluck dinners for students and families, inviting family members to gatherings with the principal, and organizing parent and family workshops. A Health Center on campus provides medical and dental services for students. The Family and College Resource Center (FRC) provides the space for many of those programs and activities:

- Four mornings a week, the FRC becomes a classroom for parents learning English through a partnership with the district's adult school. Childcare is free.
- Parents receive support on everything from navigating the school's web-based student information system to communicating with the teacher.
- Staff members connect parents to services such as tax or legal help, counseling referrals, or food assistance.
- Teachers visit students' homes, which sends a powerful message to families. Those visits help teachers better understand how to support and motivate their students.

Parents have played a pivotal role throughout CCPA's history. For example, they petitioned the district to expand CCPA to include high school and advocated to retain the adult education program on the campus. They also monitored budgeting to ensure the district provides sufficient resources for the school.

CCPA parents also led campaigns for local state and ballot measures that increased the school's budget substantially and strengthened its ability to provide high-quality programs for students. Principal Amy Carozza declared, "Without our parent community and their direct advocacy for schools in Oakland, we would not be able to improve and grow the school for the kids the way we have been over the past years" (Adapted from McLaughlin et al., 2020, *The Way We Do School*).

This chapter discusses how family engagement has the power to change entire systems. The strategies for benefiting and impacting students, families, and teachers, which we addressed in Chapters 1–3, can culminate in broader wins across the school, district, or community institutions. By exploring 14 studies, this chapter seeks to address the following questions:

- How have families and communities contributed to systemic changes in their schools?

- How does family engagement factor into wider reform efforts?

- What steps can schools and districts take to elevate family engagement as a systemwide priority?

- What supports are necessary to create a culture of family-school partnership?

The studies not only show examples of what is possible when family engagement is a priority on the system level, but also highlight components needed to make it happen in the first place. Some resemble a chicken-and-egg situation. For example, building trusting relationships between educators and families is key to fostering a school culture of family engagement. But for *all* staff to engage in this relationship-building (rather than a handful of teachers), a culture of buy-in and administrative support for family engagement is needed from the beginning.

There lies the chicken-and-egg contradiction: what comes first, trusting relationships built from the ground up or staff buy-in through top-down supports? Every school and community is different, so both scenarios can exist simultaneously. Organizational conditions make equitable family engagement possible, and family engagement leads to the implementation of those conditions. It truly is a continuous feedback cycle!

Regardless of which method comes first, the studies show how this can lead to positive change. Four big stories emerge on how family engagement influences institutions:

1. Emphasizing family engagement is necessary for systemwide success.

2. Balancing power between schools and families—with equal partnership, equity, and justice as the goal—transforms institutions.

3. Providing supports to foster family engagement helps institutions themselves begin to change.

4. Building trust with families through two-way communication is essential.

Big Story 1: Emphasizing family engagement is necessary for systemwide success.

When schools create action plans to achieve systemwide improvements, they often include important elements that relate to one another, such as high academic expectations, effective collection and use of data, professional development for staff, whole-child supports, and family partnerships. While any of those elements is helpful on its own, the synergy they create leads to an even greater impact on whole systems. This is especially the case when family engagement is prioritized. Schools that emphasize it see notable systemwide changes that go deeper than academic outcomes.

Whether it's a classroom-level initiative or as a systemwide priority, family engagement was a necessary strategy for systemwide improvement in the following studies. The schools and districts in the studies saw a range of successes, from higher academic outcomes to positive shift in the mindsets of staff members.

Partner with families to plan for students' futures.

In 2007, Carol Asher and Cindy Maguire investigated the success of a group of New York City high schools, which they referred to as Beating the Odds (BTO) schools. These 13 schools consistently enrolled classes of ninth graders with high rates of poverty and low academic outcomes, and four years later, turned them around to graduate and continue their education at rates higher than the city average. The researchers identified four areas of best practice that were essential to fostering students' academic success, all of which included keeping in close contact with families.

The partnership with families began as soon as students enrolled. Schools worked with parents to scaffold the transition into high school, emphasizing transparency and accessibility in navigating a larger school system. To ensure that students continued their education past high school graduation, BTO schools engaged parents through all four years to demystify the college admissions process through college/career prep programs.

Events were facilitated by alumni, parent coordinators, or family liaisons. Many initiatives to engage and garner feedback from families were organized and led by parents themselves. At all levels, the two-way flow of communication was key so that no student fell through the cracks. Educators approached this in several ways:

- Hosting college fairs and events in partnership with local colleges
- Facilitating parent academies to help families fill out financial aid and college application forms
- Keeping families informed about college admissions processes through advisory programs that meet several times a year.

Four Areas of Successful Practice in "Beating the Odds" Schools

- **Academic rigor:** Standards for rigor are shared across all courses. Instructional leaders visit classrooms to monitor teaching quality and course content. All students take college prep and AP classes, even those in technical and career programs. Student progress is closely tracked by teachers and parents.

- **Timely supports:** Short-term interventions such as tutoring and extended-day programs allow students to catch up quickly. Each student has an adult advisor who is the parents' primary contact. Advisors help students and families set detailed college/career goals and understand how to get there.

- **A culture of college access:** Schools make it clear to entering students and families that they offer a college/career prep program. Starting in ninth grade, counselors keep families informed about required tests and courses, the college admissions process, and financial aid applications. A "college office" gives students and families information about local colleges that are good prospects and provide help filling out applications.

- **Effective use of data:** Counselors track graduation rates, and percentages of students applying and attending two- and four-year colleges. They monitor the rates at which students take the PSAT, SAT, and ACT tests and their scores. They also keep track of graduates' experiences and retention rates in the different colleges they attend.

(Ascher and Maguire, 2007. *Beating the Odds: How thirteen NYC schools bring low-performing ninth-graders to timely graduation and college enrollment*)

By engaging parents in the college admissions process from ninth grade through graduation, BTO schools attained four-year graduation rates nearly 10 percentage points above the citywide rate. This culture of college readiness relied on high academic expectations, a network of individualized supports, and using available data to adjust supports toward above-average outcomes, especially in schools where the student poverty rate was higher than the New York City average.

Improve school culture by engaging families.

In the United Kingdom, family engagement was a key feature of the Department for Education's Achievement for All (AfA) program. This effort was designed to support school systems in enhancing opportunities for learners with special educational needs and disabilities (SEND). In their evaluation of the AfA pilot program, Neil Humphrey and Garry Squires (2011) emphasized that family engagement was integral to the success of the initiative in participating schools.

A key element of the program's success was a holistic implementation of its three strands: data tracking and targeted academic interventions, expanded extracurricular learning opportunities, and structured conversations with parents. The interweaving efforts of these three main strategies led to positive outcomes for SEND students and built sustainable systems for the sites to continue these efforts into the future.

Collaboration with parents was crucial. The structured conversations brought parents in as experts on their children. Teachers were able not only to listen to parents (rather than simply relaying information to them) but then to act on the parents' concerns and suggestions. The study found that the relationship between parents and teachers was central to a watershed of improvements across academic and non-academic outcomes. With family engagement as an inextricable piece of the AfA program, schools saw improved outcomes not just for SEND students, but for students schoolwide because of improved school culture.

Many parents began to view their child's school as a partner that listened to their views and worked in their children's best interests. Overall, the structured conversations acted as "a really good vehicle to get positive relationships going" (AfA Lead) (Humphrey & Squires, 2015, p. 57). As this culture shift spread, parents beyond the AfA cohort began to feel more encouraged to come forward and talk to teachers, leading to even greater benefits for more children.

Schools quickly drew links within and between each of the strands:

- Structured conversations were used to discuss wider outcomes, such as attendance.

- Students' positive relationships with teachers contributed to their academic progress.

- School processes and practices relating to assessment, tracking, and intervention, as well as structured conversations with parents, were associated with changes in wider outcomes, such as behavior.

- These three main strategies, particularly structured conversations, worked together to create the conditions for systemwide success (Humphrey and Squires, 2015).

Focus on building relationships.

Several school districts across the country have partnered with Parent-Teacher Home Visits (PTHV) for family engagement strategies. Participating sites agree to implement five core practices, or "non-negotiables," for the program to work as designed:

1. Visits are voluntary for both educators and families. Visits are scheduled by mutual agreement in advance of the visit.

2. Teachers are trained in how to make the visits, and compensated for their time, which is outside their school day.

3. The focus of the first visit is relationship-building, not solving academic or behavior issues. Instead, educators listen, and families discuss hopes and dreams for their children. Building on this relationship, the second visit focuses on academics.

4. Students are not targeted. All students, or a cross-section, receive a visit. There must be no stigma attached to a visit.

5. Educators conduct visits in pairs and reflect afterwards with their partners.

When schools adhered to these five practices, they began to see positive outcomes, not just in student performance, but in overall school culture. (Venkateswaran, 2018). On average, schools that carry out the PTHV program as designed see decreased rates of absenteeism and higher overall proficiency in math and ELA (Sheldon & Jung, 2018).

Recognize that family engagement is essential to school improvement.

In *Organizing Schools for Improvement: Lessons from Chicago*, Anthony Bryk and his colleagues examined data from nearly 400 public elementary schools. When examining data for schools that had substantially improved, they found these schools had five "essential supports:"

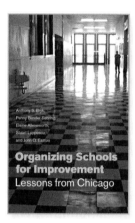

1. **Coherent instructional guidance system:** Curriculum, learning materials, support for quality instruction, emphasis on critical thinking, and a local community of practice.

2. **Professional capacity:** Quality of faculty (experience and educational background), professional development rated highly by teachers, willingness to try out new ideas, and the ability to work together to improve instruction and help colleagues do their best.

3. **Strong parent-community-school ties:** Teachers' knowledge of the community and use of local community resources; outreach to parents; inviting parents into classroom; and embracing parents as partners in improving learning.

4. **Student-centered learning climate:** A safe and orderly environment focused on learning; high expectations for students; rigorous academic work combined with extra support for struggling students; and students supporting each other.

5. **Leadership as the driver of change:** Resources provided by administrators to support quality instruction and cultivate a growing cadre of leaders (teachers, parents, and community members) who can help expand the reach of this work.

In schools identified as having strong ties to families, teachers welcomed and involved parents in their children's learning and developed more trusting relationships with parents. This emphasis on family engagement extended into other supports as well—successful school leadership worked to improve family involvement, and community representatives worked with staff to develop school improvement plans (Bryk et al., 2010).

For example, in some schools sampled in this study, improved student attendance over time strengthened their ties to parents and community. Those ties became a core resource to establish safety and order across the school. This growing sense of routine and security enhanced a better-aligned curriculum that continually exposed students to new tasks and ideas. Interesting and engaging teaching that gave students active learning roles in the classroom motivated them to learn. High-quality professional development helped teachers conduct such activities and engage parents more effectively. This combination of supports produced the conditions to improve student attendance (Bryk et al., 2010).

Overall, schools that exhibited most of the essential supports were 10 times more likely to improve than those with weak supports (Bryk et al.). This includes the strong culture of family engagement. When schools and districts commit to building reciprocal, relational trust with families at all levels—from the classroom to the central office—they see notable improvements. All the strategic pieces for improvement worked together to produce tremendous outcomes, with parent-school-community ties acting as a necessary component for success.

Big Story 2: Balancing power between schools and families—with equal partnership, equity, and justice as the goal—transforms institutions.

When family engagement is an institutional priority—and adequate supports and resources are in place to make it happen at all levels and families are welcomed as equal partners in planning and decision-making—the seeds of systemic change germinate and take root. Equitable collaboration with families that works toward goals for systemic change can transform districts.

As we've seen in previous chapters, schools have historically been marginalizing institutions—places where parents can be haunted by their own traumatic experiences—that leave parents out of decision-making or actively push parents away, that prioritize professional expertise, and that do not reflect the diversity of the communities they serve. Instead, by engaging families with trust, dignity, and a spirit of partnership, schools can work to become grounded institutions, or "schools that are rooted in and reflect the full lives and experiences of students' families and communities" (Hong, 2019, p. 160). One way this type of equitable engagement has been realized—balancing the power between schools and communities—is through community organizing efforts.

Build power in the community.

Accountability and support from outside the district or school can act as a catalyst for change. A 2009 study by the Annenberg Institute for School Reform showed that community organizing, when pursued in a district over time with intensity and at sufficient scale, can lead to big improvements in student outcomes. The study found that schools engaged with community organizing groups had better attendance, improved test scores, more students completing high school, and increased college aspirations. The Annenberg study also documented the effects of community organizing on creating equity-oriented change in school district policy, practices, and distribution of resources. At the level of individual schools, the Annenberg study also showed how organizing strengthened school-community relationships, parent involvement and engagement, and cultivated trust. (Mediratta, Shah, and McAlister, 2009. *Building partnerships to reinvent school culture: Austin Interfaith*.)

Transformed Institutions

The transformation of individuals and communities leads to institutional change in public education. Through engagement, institutions are more responsive to community concerns, encourage community participation, and are more accountable to community members. *A Match on Dry Grass* argues that community organizing offers a powerful alternative to the top-down, expert-driven approach to typical educational reform efforts (Warren & Mapp, 2011). These efforts work to improve not only public education, but the larger inequities that surround and influence it—building community capacity and the power to bring about systemic change.

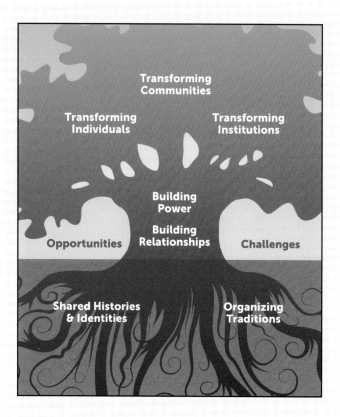

One example is Austin Interfaith, an organizing group in Texas that builds local networks of faith-based institutions and community members to improve local neighborhoods. Aiming to improve low-performing schools in East Austin, Austin Interfaith created a network of "Alliance Schools" in low-income neighborhoods. Using community organizing strategies, Austin Interfaith provided leadership training to parents, teachers, and administrators, and developed a strong relationship with the superintendent.

This organizing started with individual and small-group meetings with residents, facilitating relationship-building and forging solidarity around common concerns. In addition to mobilizing parents and supporting East Austin schools, Austin Interfaith organized at the district level: engaging with the school board and leading administrators, hosting regular "accountability sessions" between parents, school leaders, and public officials, and meeting with district staff and school board members to recruit them as allies.

Through those efforts, Austin Interfaith and community members made an impact on the district, schools, and students.

- District staff became more aware of the needs of low-income Black and Latinx communities in East Austin.

- Grant funding enabled high-poverty schools to add bilingual and special education teachers, add a parent support specialist, expand summer and adult ESL programs, and provide more professional development for educators.

- School climate and professional culture improved, and parents reported better access to information and relationships with staff.

- Student performance on state tests improved from four percentage points in schools with minimal involvement to over 15 points in schools with high involvement (p. 29).

These institutional changes were the result of a reflexive relationship between Austin schools and Austin Interfaith. As the then-superintendent of Austin ISD, Pascal Forgione, noted:

> *"Austin Interfaith has got to be my critical friend. They're not my best friend. They've got to be critical. They've got to be the conscience of my community. Sometimes I don't want to hear it; most times I don't mind because we have such shared values. But whether I like it or not, that's their job"* (p. 16).

Move beyond engagement to equitable partnerships.

Grounded institutions celebrate the diversity of communities by *connecting* with families to create a unique educational experience, rather than expecting them to assimilate into existing school norms. This begins with welcoming families as equal partners and stepping into uncertainty together to build something new and reflective of the community, working hard to not fall back into familiar and traditional power structures. In *Just Schools: Building Equitable Collaborations Between Schools and Families,* Dr. Ann Ishimaru explores this dynamic— the distinctions between conventional partnerships and equitable collaboration—through a unique collaboration between district leaders and parent leaders in the Salem-Keizer School District in Oregon.

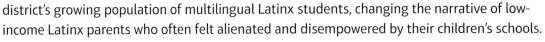

The parents and community leaders who made up the Salem-Keizer Coalition for Equality built a collaboration with district leadership to work together toward shifting practices and school culture. The Coalition wanted an educational experience that better supported the district's growing population of multilingual Latinx students, changing the narrative of low-income Latinx parents who often felt alienated and disempowered by their children's schools.

District initiatives to improve multilingual student performance at Salem-Keizer through targeted intervention had not worked. Instead, the Coalition focused on the *system's* ability to better educate these students, rather than placing the blame on students and families. They emphasized the importance of mutual accountability while the new superintendent worked to shift district culture from that of blame and denial to collective responsibility for the success of all students.

Ishimaru emphasizes how a key factor in this situation was the transformation of power, "targeting the inequitable power that lives in schooling structures, routines, policies, and everyday relations, rather than trying to change individuals or groups of people to better conform to an existing oppressive system" (p. 52). Also notable was the shared accountability and power between parents and school leaders—it's not a simple flipping of the power dynamic to put parents in control, but rather a shared and collaborative relationship between the two parties.

By moving past technical reforms and into systemic conditions—in this case, interrogating racism in school structures and in the broader community—the Coalition and Salem-Keizer School District *leaned into* larger political dynamics and challenged them within their own

Data Carousel: Data Inquiry for Equitable Collaboration

Another example of this collective inquiry in action is through the "data carousel," a model for gathering and interpreting data for transformative change. It outlines steps for "moving from data *about* students and families or families as a *source* of data to family *agency* and *leadership* in joint inquiry for improving and transforming organizations" (p. 119). Data

moves from acting as stagnant, cut-and-dried statistics to "a vehicle for repairing and building politicized trust and fostering transformative agency. These approaches open the door to exploring, defining, and pursuing more ambitious aims of holistic human flourishing, community-determined well-being, and educational justice" (p. 119).

2. PRIORITIZE
What data or process will best help us attend to equity and answer our questions?

1. QUESTION
Convene a leadership group to initiate the process. Why are we doing this? Who do we need to work with? What questions do we have, and how will we use what we learn?

3. ENGAGE
Draw on cultural brokers and existing leaders to reach out to stakeholder groups and invite their participation.

4. MAKE SENSE
Share data. Collaborate with stakeholders to make sense of it. What does the data tell us? What other questions do we have?

Data Inquiry for Equitable Collaboration

5. STRATEGIZE
Reconvene and expand leadership group. What did we learn? What are the next steps?

6. ACT
Change policies or practices. Leverage new relationships. Discover new questions for further inquiry.

Adapted from "Data Inquiry for Equitable Collaboration: The Case of Neighborhood House's Data Carousel" copyright © 2015 by University of Washington.

system. Typically, these dynamics are avoided, deemed uncomfortable by school staff, and brushed aside to maintain perceived peace. But what happens in a school is inextricably linked to the sociopolitical context of its community, meaning that "the generative power of district-community (or school-family) collaboration lies in *how* actors engage the inevitable tensions in these 'new relationships'" (p. 54). This goal of systemic change means that equitable collaborations are not static—they are a constant process of collective inquiry, a learning process for all involved to engage in healthy relational and political tensions "that can open up new ways forward that we otherwise might not have imagined" (p. 54).

These approaches decenter educators' agendas not just by engaging parents in their children's education, but by *partnering* with families to create an environment that builds and reflects on the cultural experiences and values of a school's community. This means moving beyond simply supporting school-based activities and events toward collaborating with parents to bring their knowledge and expertise into the equation. But it is important to always continue the process of collective inquiry—a perpetual feedback loop to examine and interrogate typical power dynamics when they inevitably reemerge.

Another way to incorporate these principles is through solidarity-driven co-design, which "aims to foster solidarities through collective inquiry by explicitly addressing and working to reconstruct how historically rooted power plays out in the process of co-constructing new knowledge and implementing change" (p. 142). Rather than following the logic that families need to be changed or educated to better support their children's education, co-design is a "process that cultivates the collective learning of *both* families *and* educators" (p. 153). For example, the Family Leadership Design Collective (FLDC) worked with four sites in major cities across the country to facilitate co-design initiatives. This included the community organizing group CADRE in South Los Angeles, which partnered with UCLA to co-design role-plays to develop new scripts for humanizing parent-teacher interactions and building solidarities among BIPOC (Black, Indigenous, people of color) parents in LAUSD.

Balance top-down and ground-up.

Many transformative family engagement initiatives happen when ground-up efforts work together with top-down supports. One method of providing top-down, system-level support from outside of a school district is a cross-sector collaboration: a network of stakeholders that provide support and resources to schools and their communities. One example of a cross-sector collaboration that worked to benefit schools from Ann Ishimaru's 2019 study was the Pathways Project (a pseudonym for the organization used in the study), a cross-sector collaboration that brought together education, community, health services, and other organizational partners to support a region of suburban poverty in the Western U.S. Theoretically, this collaboration and others like it seem the ideal context for building authentic networks for engagement and leveraging the political will for sustained change. At the same time, however, it came with its own limitations that inhibited change.

Co-design through the lens of district leadership, as detailed in *Just Schools*:

"**Kelly,** an Asian American man, was an executive director (principal supervisor) in his large urban district. A former principal and teacher, he strongly identified as an equity-focused leader and oversaw 20 high-poverty schools in the region of the city with the most diverse student body in the district. His co-design work shifted from supporting an embattled principal in repairing family-school relations to teaching principals how to begin co-design and, ultimately, to partnering with a school community and the district director of racial equity in a process to hire a new principal at one school.

Justin, a gay White man, was the assistant superintendent of elementary instruction and equity in a suburban district with a growing (mostly immigrant) student of color population. He began with the ambition of "leading up" to co-design the district's strategic plan implementation and improvement process, then shifted to developing a family engagement policy to better leverage his existing relationships and points of leverage in his system. He eventually focused on an existing district community advisory group that had become somewhat entrenched and disgruntled. With several key district staff members and families, they co-designed a new selection process, charge, and operating norms to reshape the role and focus of the district community advisory group in relation to the core equity work of the district.

Keisha, an African American woman, was executive director of organizational development and equity in a diverse urban district. A former principal with deep ties in the community, she partnered with the local housing authority and with African American and East African families, initially to address chronic absenteeism among students in one housing authority development. Early on, the leadership team shifted to co-designing a program to address family priorities to improve the educational experiences of their youth. The project also attempted to address interracial tensions between these two communities. The team drew on an existing $15,000 grant to ultimately co-design a youth mentoring program with a family engagement component."

—Adapted from Ishimaru, 2020, pp. 143–144

Three initiatives within the collaboration, two school-based and one neighborhood-based, were identified by the Pathways Project for their leadership in parent engagement and received funding and support to further improve their programming. Dr. Ishimaru investigated the cross-sector collaboration and its selected initiatives to see how the wider organization facilitated (or hindered) equitable collaboration with families, particularly looking for practices that shared power more equally between families and schools.

While the Pathways Project intended to facilitate systemic change through top-down support and resources, some disconnects bubbled up in the relationship between stakeholders and on-the-ground initiatives. The initiatives found themselves competing against each other for resources, constraining their ability to challenge power structures with transformative practices. One participant coined the term "collabetition" to describe how, while stakeholders were all working toward a common vision, "the structures and mechanisms in the initiative created a sense of constant competition for financial and human resources, media attention, priorities, and opportunities for many of the project partners" (p. 376).

This shows how delicate the balance is between top-down and ground-up strategies working together for equitable family engagement: A lack of top-down strategies can limit the scale and reach of family partnerships throughout the system, and a lack of ground-up strategies can prevent transformative change and relationship-building. Adequate supports are essential to facilitate this work, especially those that prepare educators to meet families on equal ground.

Big Story 3: Providing supports to foster family engagement helps institutions themselves begin to change.

When family engagement is central to school-improvement efforts, especially with relationships built from the ground up, schools see a cascade of improvements, from a more welcoming culture to higher academic outcomes. For these practices to be sustainable and far-reaching, school systems have implemented key supports for staff at all levels, from teachers in the classroom up to administrators in the district central office. Those supports include capacity-building—training for educators and staff to engage families effectively—as well as funding for training, necessary resources, program activities, and fair compensation. Supports must also be relational: Teachers and families must support each other, school administrators must support teachers, district administrators support school administrators, and local government and organizations must support the district. When people at each level have the supports they need to succeed, their actions generate buy-in for family engagement across the system.

Encourage families to talk to their children about learning.

Gillian Baxter and Dianne Toe examined family engagement through social media in three Australian primary schools. They learned how effective online platforms can be in building the capacity of parents to connect with and support their children's learning. Social media posts encouraged parent engagement by asking for families to comment and share their own knowledge and experiences with education, rather than just relaying information to them. In one case, students exercised agency by sharing their own learnings on the platforms with posts that explained concepts they were learning in class and their problem-solving process.

The study found that, through the critical participatory action research process, online methods moved from informing parents through an online space to facilitating conversations about learning, and then creating a shared dialogue between families and school. To achieve this shift from involvement to engagement, school leaders worked closely with teachers to identify strengths and areas for improvement in developing more accessible, interactive social media posts to engage families.

As one school leader in the study emphasized, family engagement is "all about reinforcing parents' capacity to have learning conversations with their children" (Baxter & Toe, 2021, p. 19). Teachers and school leaders worked together to build the capacity of parents to contribute to a reflexive, shared learning space with comments and insights. School leaders provided frequent support to teachers to continuously adapt online engagement methods based on parent feedback. These were emphasized as add-in, rather than add-on, work—shifts in practice to incorporate critical inquiry *into* daily work, rather than tack on as *more* work for teachers.

Routine practices underwent fundamental change. One participant noted that "as a leader there are times that you have got to be very explicit in supporting teachers, and through my role, I'm explicitly teaching about family school partnerships" (Baxter & Tow, 2021, p. 19). This administrative support and scaffolding for helping teachers engage families builds toward an institutional culture of home-school partnership.

Build in supports for school practice at the district level.

Parent-Teacher Home Visits are successful not just for their emphasis on relationship-building, but also because they include the supports necessary to make transformative practices possible. Participating districts host a PTHV coordinator, who acts as both an advocate for the program at the district level and an administrator, who supports school-based coordinators. Successful programs require this position along with a close coordination of other staff— principals, PTHV coordinators, as well as family liaisons. School staff further hold regular meetings to reflect on and learn from experiences in the program.

This close-knit network generates supports from all sides: PTHV coordinators and district administrators provide support for and promote buy-in with participating schools. The principals of those schools actively support school staff in their family engagement efforts. Teachers support family members so they feel more comfortable with the home visits. When all these supports are in place, they build a school culture of family engagement. Parents not only expect a home visit, but readily ask educators when they will be coming for one (Venkateswaran, 2018).

Another crucial relationship is district support of on-site administrators, particularly in districts implementing external reforms. When family partnerships are a priority at the central office, adequate supports for principals can help to foster buy-in at school sites. In her 2014 study, Mavis Sanders examined two districts supporting multiple sites in their implementation of a family-school-community engagement reform developed by the National Network of Partnership Schools (NNPS). This system-level, top-down approach cultivated a network of active supports, particularly through NNPS coordinators, who were essential to developing partnership programs.

What do Network for Partnership Coordinators do?

- Lead professional development sessions with school personnel
- Build relationships with parents, local businesses, and community organizations
- Model collaborative behaviors
- Emphasize partnerships as part of principals' goals for school improvement and student learning (Sanders, 2014).

Good leadership is key for successful family-school partnerships. This means strong leadership by principals at the school site and by administrators at the central office. Principals embraced the NNPS reform to improve school climate, grades, and attendance, and teachers working with them reported a clear understanding of their values on family partnerships. When principals in this study valued family-school-community partnerships, they were more likely to engage in activities that welcomed families and communities. These included:

- Creating "welcoming school" environments

- Collaborating with community-based organizations to engage ethnically and linguistically diverse families

- Allocating funds for and attending family and community partnership activities

- Acknowledging parent and teacher leadership for family and community engagement (Sanders, 2014, p. 247).

This buy-in among staff didn't occur overnight, however—it was facilitated by NNPS coordinators with the support of district administration. The key factors that bolstered these supports and sustained buy-in were accountability measures—including family engagement metrics as part of principal evaluations—and recognition, publicly celebrating partnership efforts and achievements. When family engagement is a priority at the system level, with districts providing adequate supports and accountability measures for educators, schools begin to see an effective combination of ground-up and top-down efforts.

Recognize that transformation requires buy-in at all levels.

Leadership-driven buy-in was also a key factor for success in Beating the Odds schools. These schools achieved their successful turnarounds with students through the hard work and leadership of staff and administrators at each site—however, their innovations were not a district initiative. In fact, they often had to take professional risks and challenge broader institutional mandates—from the district up to the federal level—to do what was needed. When one BTO principal was asked whether there was a way to do all of this without being a hero or a heroine, she responded with a strong "No!" When exhaustion threatened, she explained, her recourse was to ask herself and her staff, "Wouldn't you do this for your own child?" (Ascher & Maguire, 2007, p. 14).

These leaders' efforts highlight how a strong focus on family engagement both impacts and can be impeded by institutions. BTO schools' success showed how this commitment benefited school sites, and it underscored how institutions above the school level can better facilitate this work: giving high schools more access to resources, greater control to maintain smaller enrollments, recognition for success, and a more robust system of support and accountability from the district. Despite barriers and challenges, BTO educators pushed themselves to do the best for students and their families and saw a wide range of positive impacts as a result.

Facilitate social connections.

Another important resource, in line with relational trust, is social capital. In their 2010 study of Chicago schools, *Organizing Schools for Improvement*, Bryk and colleagues found that neighborhood social capital was an invaluable resource for improving local schools. Close-knit networks of community ties and resources were more likely in areas where residents had a history of working together. In communities where residents were more alienated, improvement efforts were more likely to stagnate. When communities with significant social capital also had strong institutions, especially religious institutions, these were very supportive contexts for school improvement. These institutions foster networks of social ties and have connections that can bring outside resources into isolated neighborhoods (Bryk et al., 2010).

What Is Social Capital?

Social capital is the goodwill, sympathy, and connections created by social interaction within and between people and their social networks.

Improving schools can be found in all kinds of neighborhoods, but truly disadvantaged communities present their own unique challenges. In *Organizing Schools for Improvement*, stagnating reform efforts piled up in very poor, racially isolated Black neighborhoods. The authors note the following:

> *The essential supports must be very strong for significant improvement in student learning to occur in truly disadvantaged communities where social capital is scarce. This finding raises troublesome questions about our society's capacity to improve schools in its most neglected communities. For these school communities, it is a "three strike" problem. Not only are the schools highly stressed…but they exist in weak communities and confront an extraordinary density of human needs that walk through the front door every day* (pp. 209–210).

In this context, family-school-community ties are especially difficult to build and sustain. Bryk and colleagues recommend addressing these challenges through deeper systemic interventions: "comprehensive and integrated set of community, school, and related social program initiatives, aimed at cultivating local leadership and more productive working relationships among school staff, parents, and local neighborhood services and officials" (p. 210). These initiatives require material resources from local, state, and/or federal governments and stakeholders, as well as capacity- and relationship-building opportunities for community residents.

Address root causes of inequities.

Full-service community schools (FSCS) are an example of what Bryk and Schneider recommend. Community schools offer an "expanded vision of schooling" and operate outside traditional school structures. They see physical and mental health, safety, positive adult connections, expanded learning time, and social supports, as integral to children's learning and development. This often takes the form of a public-school building operating in partnership with community agencies. Acting as a community center, such schools welcome students and their families before and after school, often seven days a week. Community schools employ three broad approaches:

- They provide expanded learning opportunities that are motivating and engaging during the school day, after school, and in the summer.

- They offer essential health and social supports and services.

- They engage families and communities as assets in the lives of their children.

In their study, *The Way We Do School* (2020), Milbrey McLaughlin and her colleagues examined the unique community schools model in Oakland, California. The full-service community schools model contrasts sharply with the "no excuses" view that has dominated many school improvement efforts such as standards-based accountability. These models hold a deficit-based and judgmental view of families and communities, ignoring the impact of systemic inequities and institutional racism on student and school success.

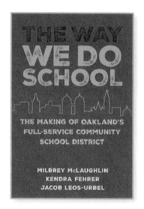

Community school efforts usually focus on improving individual schools. During the 2010s, however, the Oakland Unified School District (OUSD) set out to reorganize its entire structure into a system of full-service community schools to disrupt inequities in opportunities available to local students. This meant transforming the system, rather than approaching reform school-by-school, implementing a comprehensive web of whole-child supports as "a way of doing school." This system change was focused at two levels—the central office and local schools. Rather than locate community services in school buildings, this model integrates community resources into the school's academic program (see the opening vignette on Coliseum College Prep Academy). As the authors put it, "Oakland operates as a community school district, not as a district with some community schools" (p. ix).

In 2011, after 18 months of comprehensive planning and community engagement, OUSD Superintendent Tony Smith rolled out the *Community Schools, Thriving Students* strategic plan to kick off the path toward a FSCS district. Despite tumultuous political, social, and economic challenges over the next eight years—including five leadership turnovers and repeated budget crises—the district built and sustained a still-expanding FSCS initiative. By the 2019–20 school year, 42 of the 86 district schools were operating with a full-time community school manager. During that year, students made 36,000 visits to OUSD'S 16 school-based health centers. The district's 75 after-school programs attracted 8,000 participants every day. Partnerships with 215 community organizations have enriched the school day with a diverse array of learning opportunities. Furthermore, *all* the district's schools include core elements of a FSCS model, such as social-emotional learning strategies and Coordination of Services Teams (COST).

OUSD's systemwide FSCS initiative have benefited students in several ways:

- Reduced suspensions and high-risk behaviors

- Improved school climate and culture

- Increased family and youth involvement in site-based decisions

- Expanded mental and physical health resources leading to improved student health outcomes

- Led to high levels of participation in after-school programs (73 percent)

- Increased high school graduation rate.

The most notable impact on students is the rise in high school graduation rates, which have steadily grown by over 14 percentage points, from 59.3 percent in 2011 to 73.5 percent in 2019. Students most at risk have benefited the most.

Oakland's work to transform its entire district shows how a community school model—providing capacity building and material support for educators, families, and students—can be a framework for a systemwide change. This approach commits to tackling inequitable structures at their root, a necessary strategy for achieving systemic change. Rather than going after surface-level "problems to fix," like targeted interventions to improve academic performance, this strategy addresses systemic problems.

Disparities in resources and opportunities available to young people growing up in concentrated poverty stem from structural problems. Food insecurity, homelessness, insufficient social supports, and scant medical care, for example, cannot be solved by quick-fix, adopt-a-program responses. Furthermore, these social and economic disparities explain much of the so-called "achievement gaps" in student outcomes. In short, students struggle to learn when their basic needs are not being met.

OUSD set out to disrupt these inequities by infusing its entire district, from the central office down to school sites, with the community schools mindset. Then it provided the supports necessary to make it happen. The sustainability and success of this initiative hinged on collaboration with families—district leaders taking the time to develop a comprehensive plan *with* families, community members, and local partners. When family partnerships are a priority at all levels of the institution, schools *and* communities see deep-rooted structural change toward equity. The boundaries between a school and its neighborhood blur, allowing for two-way feedback and positive change to ripple outward. At the root of all of these efforts are the mutual understanding and trust that must be built between educators and families (McLaughlin et al., 2020).

Big Story 4: Building trust with families through two-way communication is essential.

> *Some of the most powerful relationships found in our data are associated with relational trust and how it operates as both a lubricant for organizational change and a moral resource for sustaining the hard work of local school improvement* (Bryk et al., 2010, p. 207).

In most cases, systemwide improvement begins with educators building trusting relationships with families. Those relationships grow from the ground up, with or without top-down support. Educators and families build trust through two-way communication, structured opportunities to interact, culturally relevant curriculum and instruction, and strategies that minimize barriers to engagement. When that trust is built, it acts as the foundation for systemwide buy-in and transformational change.

To engage families from the ground up, start by building relationships with families by establishing frequent, positive, and respectful two-way communication. Across the studies in this chapter, schools that began engagement efforts by building relationships with families saw systemwide changes in mindset—how teachers and administrators viewed and approached families in the communities they serve.

Recognize that trust is the soil in which improvements can germinate.

In *Trust in Schools: A Core Resource for Improvement*, Anthony S. Bryk and Barbara Schneider examined whether relational trust in schools was key to improving academic success in disadvantaged Chicago elementary schools. Relational trust was measured by reviewing teacher-parent trust, teacher-teacher trust, and teacher-principal trust. The long-term study, which analyzed data from hundreds of elementary schools, found that high levels of trust trended with the highest-achieving schools in the top fourth, and low levels of trust predicted lower student performance in the bottom fourth. These same trends appeared in schools' productivity—those with higher trust were much more likely to improve over time.

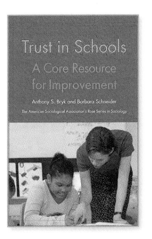

The theory of change, which the research supports, is that the amount of trust in a school affects its ability to carry out reforms. Complex reforms take time and require a level of mutual support and teamwork that trust enables. Small wins expand trust, which then increases the capacity to take on new challenges. The changes made then improve student learning (Bryk and Schneider, 2002, p. 121).

In short, we view relational trust as creating the fertile social ground for core technical resources (such as standards, assessments, and new curricula) to take root and develop into something of value. Without this, individual staff may excel at their work, certain school functions may be well executed, but the school as a social system will continue to fail many of its members (Bryk and Schneider, 2002, p. 135).

View teachers and parents as a powerful combination.

Teachers and parents can often approach each other as enemies, held back by preconceptions, insecurities, and institutional or systemic barriers that prevent equal collaboration. This is particularly the case for many nondominant families (those impacted by systemic oppression), who may not share the cultural and social norms typically valued in U.S. school systems, which tend to cater to White, upper-middle class mores. In her book *Natural Allies: Hope and Possibility in Teacher-Family Partnerships*, Soo Hong (2019) explores what can happen when educators take the time to build trust with all families. The teachers shifted their mindsets as they came to approach families on equal ground, working to understand their backgrounds and values through effective two-way communication.

These efforts are encouraging—they highlight the potential for educators and staff across a school or district to practice relationship-building with families, beyond just a handful of teachers. If this commitment to building understanding and trust between teachers and parents became a systemwide effort, imagine the breadth of partnership outcomes on the institutional level. Benefits include more than just test scores or data outcomes—educators may change their attitudes and perceptions, thereby changing their practice as well. When enough educators undergo such a shift, family partnerships can impact a whole institution.

As discussed earlier, building relationships is at the core of Parent-Teacher Home Visits. The first visit to a family's home is reserved for getting to know families, their values, and their hopes and dreams for their children—no academic shop talk until a good rapport is established. This practice is a central tenet of the PTHV program. Schools that adhere to this emphasis on initial relationship-building, together with the other core practices of the program, see marked success in school culture and outcomes for students. (Venkateswaran, 2018)

Achievement for All leveraged this importance of building organic relationships between educators and families by implementing structured conversations between teachers and parents as a fundamental part of the program. This helped teachers to better understand students and their backgrounds, as well as develop shared goals and cooperation between school and home. An emphasis on two-way communication, on building these authentic relationships, was integral to the success of the program in participating schools. Parents had a better understanding of what went on at school, and teachers better understood what went on at home, allowing for a more cooperative, shared space between the two.

This collaboration, carried out by educators throughout AfA schools, helped to shift mindsets and school culture toward better opportunities for SEND students. It was also key to the sustainability of the program. Over 90 percent of schools indicated their intention to continue the structured conversations after the pilot, and several operated with a "sustainability mentality" from the outset (Humphrey and Squires, 2011, p. 61). In several cases, AfA schools worked toward sustainability by providing the necessary material and capacity-building supports, such as long-term funding, and focusing on bolstering practices not dependent on funding, such as a school culture of awareness and focus on SEND (Humphrey and Squires, 2011).

As Bryk and Schneider conclude in *Trust in Schools*:

> *Good schools are intrinsically social enterprises that depend heavily on cooperative endeavors among the varied participants who comprise the school community. Relational trust constitutes the connective tissue that binds these individuals together around advancing the education and welfare of children. Improving schools requires us to think harder about how best to organize the work of the adults and students so that this connective tissue remains healthy and strong.* (p. 144)

Conclusion

In school systems where family engagement is an ongoing priority, change ripples out from the building into the wider community. Schools must welcome these changes and continue to tackle the systemic inequities that act as barriers to engagement. For that to happen, educators and their schools must decenter their agendas to co-create an educational experience that reflects the community they work in and build authentic relationships with their students' families. The key to sustainable, systemic change in institutions is not checking boxes in a school improvement plan, but rather working toward true systemic change. The road to educational justice begins with equitable family partnerships. Rather than viewing families as people who need fixing (i.e., assimilate to established norms), these partnerships collaborate with families to level power dynamics, address systemic racism, and open the system to full, equal, and equitable participation.

CHAPTER 5

IMPLICATIONS FOR PRACTICE:
Acting on the Research

High-impact family engagement is transformative work. As we note in the introduction, it leads to positive changes in beliefs and mindsets: When families, educators, students, and communities work together and develop trust, they come to understand each other's humanity, which leads to an equity-driven school culture. We hope this book can provide the ammunition you need to persuade your colleagues, funders, public officials, and others in your orbit to move forward with these evidence-based practices and transform your schools, districts, and communities.

Ultimately, the 40 research studies presented in Chapters 1 to 4 confirm what we know: school-family partnerships are essential for student success. Here's a recap.

- Chapter 1 discussed the benefits of family engagement practices on student outcomes. For instance, the chapter noted how creating seamless pathways for families to navigate the system, from pre-K through high school, is essential for student academic and social-emotional well-being.

- Chapter 2 discussed how developing trusting and authentic relationships between families and educators positively shifts educators' mindsets and approaches they may make to their students' families.

- Chapter 3 elaborated on the "family" side of family-school partnerships by unpacking the importance of family engagement practices for the families themselves. Those practices, studies show, can develop families' sense of self-efficacy in supporting their children's education and develop family leaders.

- Chapter 4 explored the benefits of family engagement practices on schools, districts, and communities. Research shows that in school systems where family engagement is an ongoing, reflexive practice toward educational and social justice, instead of a means to an end, its benefits proliferate out to the community level. Just as schools become more welcoming, so do communities.

The studies illustrate how family engagement practices benefit all involved: students, educators, family members, and communities. Across all four chapters, major findings include:

1. Strong, trusting relationships among families, schools, and communities lay the foundation for all other efforts to succeed.

2. Authentic two-way communication is key to developing trusting relationships and deeper understanding.

3. Family-school-community partnerships can be transformative at both the personal and institutional levels.

4. Meaningful family engagement practice must be systemic and sustained through resources, leadership, support, and infrastructure.

5. When family engagement is a core value of school systems, it is a powerful equity strategy.

To underscore the importance of establishing trusting relationships and true partnerships, first we align the major findings with the Dual Capacity-Building Framework for Family-School

Partnerships (Version 2) (DCBF) (Mapp & Bergman, 2019). This tool supports the development of family engagement strategies, policies, and programs. There are strong connections between the major findings presented in this book and the DCBF's essential conditions for successful partnerships presented.

From there, we recommend practices based on the findings that serve as a call to action. Now that we have reviewed the research, what can be done with the information? In other words, how do we apply what we've learned from research to family engagement practices? Our recommended practices include:

1. Intentionally cultivate relationships of trust and respect.

2. Start family engagement practices early.

3. Communicate clearly and continuously.

4. Focus on equity.

5. Prepare educators at all levels to work with families.

6. Extend networks and partnerships.

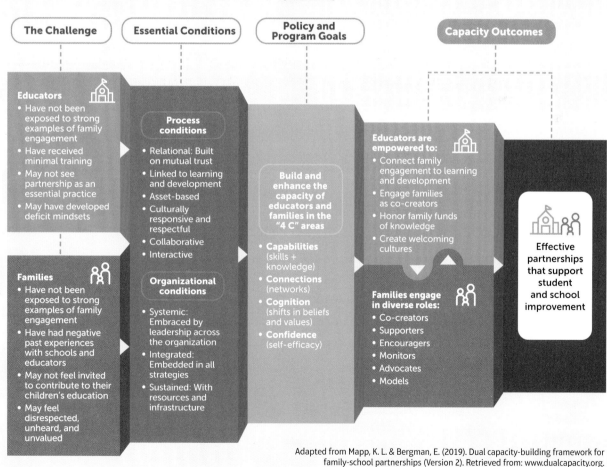

The Dual Capacity-Building Framework for Family-School Partnerships
(Version 2)

Adapted from Mapp, K. L. & Bergman, E. (2019). Dual capacity-building framework for family-school partnerships (Version 2). Retrieved from: www.dualcapacity.org.

Essential Conditions for Successful Family Engagement: Major Findings

The DCBF identifies "essential conditions" for successful family engagement practices, initiatives, and policies, consisting of process and organizational conditions. The process conditions call for practices, initiatives, and policies to be:

- Relational (built on mutual trust)
- Developmental and linked to learning
- Asset-based
- Culturally responsive and respectful
- Collaborative
- Interactive

The organizational conditions highlight the importance of leadership and resources within organizations, noting that practices, initiatives, and policies must be:

- Systemic: embraced by leaderships across the organization
- Integrated: embedded in all strategies
- Sustained: with resources and infrastructure

Major Finding 1: Strong, trusting relationships among families, schools, and communities lay the foundation for all other efforts to succeed.

The research presented in this book affirms the importance and power of relationships in family engagement work. It also makes clear that the nature of the relationships is a critical consideration. In other words, it is not enough to have open lines of communication between families and educators. Relational trust—consisting of the elements of respect, competence, integrity, and personal regard for others—must be established and nurtured to maximize the effects of that communication (Bryk & Schneider, 2002).

Furthermore, strong trusting relationships activate shifts in beliefs, mindsets, and practices of educators and families: families and educators view one another through an asset-based lens, empathize with one another, and value each other's humanity. Strong trusting relationships also help educators understand families' daily realities and their challenges to engagement, information they can use to inform their family engagement practices.

The earlier relationships are established, the better. When educators partner with families early in their children's school years, they are more likely to continue that partnership. Furthermore, the research demonstrates that strong trusting relationships have positive implications for students' academic outcomes over time.

Major Finding 2: Authentic two-way communication is key to developing trusting relationships and deeper understanding.

Communication between families and teachers has a positive impact on students' development and academic achievements. However, that communication must be authentic, meaning it must be clear, reciprocal, consistent, ongoing, and accessible. It must also be culturally responsive and respectful: School personnel need to communicate with families in multiple languages and avoid using intimidating jargon. They must take on a listening stance, creating space for all voices to be heard, and reflect cultural norms and values when communicating with families. Furthermore, the research shows that families may want to engage in their children's education but lack the tools or information to do so. Thus, the information shared with them should explicitly be linked to their children's learning and development, with clear directions on what families should do to support children's learning.

Major Finding 3: Family-school-community partnerships can be transformative at both the personal and institutional level.

In addition to benefiting students' academic outcomes, family engagement also benefits their social-emotional well-being. In distressed communities, radical healing—the process of restoring hope through empowerment—supports students' ability to resolve conflicts and promotes healthy relationships.

Family engagement can also positively impact educators and families themselves. The research presented in this book demonstrates that it can shift educators' beliefs, mindsets, and practices. Research also shows that when families take part in leadership training, or collaborate in initiatives to improve schools, it strengthens their sense of self-efficacy and ability to lead. In other words, when schools share power with families, families become empowered to support their children's learning and improve school environments.

Family engagement not only leads to improved outcomes for individual students, educators, and families themselves, but the collective as well. Family engagement practices need to be integrated. When families are empowered to engage in their children's education, and community organizations are involved, student outcomes drastically improve. Thus, it is essential that family engagement also integrates community engagement, when possible, working and partnering with local entities, such as businesses, healthcare providers, and parks and recreation offices.

Major Finding 4: Meaningful family engagement practice must be systemic and sustained through resources, leadership, support, and infrastructure.

To ensure student, family, educator, and community transformation, family engagement practices need to be given the human and financial resources to make them happen. They need to be sustained through a commitment to provide the leadership, infrastructure, and training support at all levels of the system. Furthermore, the research shows the importance of sustaining family engagement throughout students' pre-K–12 trajectories. While the nature of family engagement shifts as students move up the grades, family-school partnerships remain essential.

Major Finding 5: When family engagement is a core value of school systems, it is a powerful equity strategy.

Family engagement practices are equity strategies. When families are seen and treated as true and equal partners, equity efforts take into consideration the needs of all—students, families, educators, and community members. To benefit from the promise of family engagement practices to impact equity efforts, family engagement needs to be a systemwide value. The commitment to create a culture of partnership needs to be systemic. For that to happen, initiatives need to be supported by organizational leaders. In other words, teachers and other educators who work one-on-one with students and families should not be the only ones prioritizing relationships with families. To be fully realized, family engagement and equity practices need to be integrated, cultivated, and supported by school and community leaders.

Moving Forward: Recommended Practices

Now that we have covered what the research says about the benefits and impact of family engagement practices, let's consider what to do with its findings. As we reflect on those findings, it is important to think about the goals of family engagement practices: to welcome and partner with families, especially diverse and nondominant families. If we are serious about overcoming educational inequities, including racial and socioeconomic inequities, we must intentionally partner with families.

Recommendation 1: Intentionally cultivate relationships of trust and respect.

- **Establish trust and center efforts on children's learning and healthy development.** Ensure that school leaders understand that close and continuous parent-teacher collaboration, based on trust and respect, is essential for student progress. Honoring families' cultures and knowledge allows teachers to deepen their cultural competence, build on families' strengths, and help students appreciate their classmates' diverse backgrounds. Home visits, virtual check-ins, and regular two-way conversations about their children's learning validate parents as experts on their children and show you value them as partners. Those practices also help to correct the power imbalance that can undermine trust. Teachers can also use text messaging, social media, and Internet Parent Portals (such as PowerSchool) to keep two-way communication flowing.

- **Include family partnerships in school-improvement plans that center justice as the long-term goal.** While shorter-term, concrete goals such as raising academic outcomes and increasing student attendance are important for tracking progress, they should not be viewed as ends in themselves. True partnerships between families and schools must be a major part of long-term improvement plans, especially those focused on systemic change and social justice. Intentionally including families in these plans further establishes trust, respect, and buy-in.

Recommendation 2: Start family engagement practices early.

- **Start when children are young and equip families to navigate the system.** When children enter a quality early childhood program at age three, they engage in activities that promote their academic and social development, and their caregivers gain skills to encourage their learning. In addition, families develop relationships with other families and teachers and connect to community resources, extending their pool of resources. Families also learn how the education system works and how to express their ideas and concerns to teachers and other staff members, enabling them to advocate and problem-solve for their children and other families' children.

- **Welcome families at the beginning of the school year.** Reach out to families at the beginning of the school year in a welcoming and inviting manner. That can be done through phone calls or videoconferences in which teachers introduces themselves to families. When families feel welcomed and invited, they are more likely to trust their children's teachers and be willing to communicate. When trust is established, families begin to share their realities, dreams, and aspirations for their children, and possible barriers to engagement. As a result, they become better-informed supporters of their children's learning and monitors of their progress.

- **Continue engaging families up to college and career.** Partner with students and families *throughout* the student's educational trajectory: Family engagement practices should occur at all levels of students' education, from early childhood programs to postsecondary institutions (e.g., college and universities and career training programs). Transitions between schools should be seamless. Develop relationships with feeder schools to make the transition as smooth as possible for families.

For example, elementary schools should partner with their local middle schools and connect fifth grade families to the middle school staff. Middle schools should do the same with their respective high schools. Additionally, as students move through the educational system, the nature of family engagement practices needs to shift to meet their developmental need. As students get older, invite them to have an active role in their education. Student-led conferences are a great opportunity to empower students to share their academic progress with their educators and families.

Recommendation 3: Communicate clearly and continuously.

- **Establish ongoing two-way communication with families.** Clear, frequent, and continuous communication between families and educators is essential to developing relational trust and strong partnerships. Families want the information they need to support and monitor their children's learning in real time. That information can include notices of upcoming events, updates on their children's academic progress, and details about curriculum, to name a few.

- **Make information accessible.** Information needs to be shared in an accessible manner, meaning it's important to think about the language and platform in which it's shared. Technology, including social media, makes it easy to communicate with families on a regular basis. Yet, it is important to remember that not all families have access to reliable technology or feel comfortable using it. Language translations should be mindfully revised and edited: Sometimes direct translations (such as the ones provided by the Google translates website) are not correct.

- **Link communications to what students are learning.** Develop an open, ongoing dialogue between teachers and parents about children's learning. These three steps allow the partnership to flourish: develop a collaborative relationship and listen actively to parents, focus on supporting critical skills, and co-develop with families a plan for collaborating. With this level of guidance, parents of all backgrounds can support learning at home. These steps can be used, for example, in parent-teacher conferences (or better yet, student-led conferences), workshops, and Zoom check-ins with families. Use social media or SMS messaging to relay tips to families. Be sure the messages support home learning, are linked to what children are learning and doing in class, invite two-way communication, and are written in the families' home language. Adding a personal phone call to communicate about the student's progress can yield even greater gains.

Recommendation 4: Focus on equity.

- **Provide extra supports so that all families get what they need to support their children's learning.** Ensure that schools, especially those in low-income neighborhoods, have the resources to help families and students to deal with trauma and deprivation, and to build on their strengths. Consider creating family resource centers that offer childcare, referrals to social services and healthcare, GED and English language programs, parent/student leadership training, and other resources that would benefit families. Equip school social workers to organize and lead healing circles and other services to address trauma, and teachers to organize and lead inquiry circles to address implicit bias and structural racism. Begin circles with social-emotional check-ins. Develop an advisory system to ensure that middle and high school parents are in regular contact with someone who knows their child well. Offer after-school programs to provide extended learning time and a way for parents, teachers, and students to connect. Expand learning opportunities by partnering with community organizations to provide social services and after-school and summer programs.

- **Design family engagement practices that consider the realities of family life, such as childcare, work constraints, and the need to feed family members.** When planning family engagement activities such as open houses, parent-teacher conferences, and college application workshops, consider how to make them as inclusive as possible. For example, if a significant number of parents have a 9-to-5 job, hold events on weekends. If families need transportation to and from events, consider providing bus vouchers or moving the events to a more central location. That is why getting to know families is essential: We learn about their constraints and can address them.

- **Share power with families.** Through collective inquiry and continuous learning, schools can work with families and communities to improve outcomes, relationships, and school culture. They can work towards educational equity, building a school environment that reflects the culture and values of its community by having everyone's knowledge and expertise at play. Invite families to be decision-makers. Inviting families to co-create schoolwide plans and implementation strategies make the work easier and more successful: Families come to understand the importance of social justice and equity ideas. Also, when you share power with families in those ways, families model good citizenship for their children, family members, and neighbors.

Recommendation 5: Prepare educators at all levels to work with families.

- **Provide all educators with professional development on family engagement.**
Educators (including teachers, school and district leaders, school counselors, and other program administrators and staff) need to develop the capacity to work with families. Therefore, they need to be trained on how to communicate authentically with families and develop relationships with them. School leaders need to make time and space for professional development that centers family engagement practices. For example, teachers and staff can be coached on how to take an asset-based stance in their first meeting or phone call with families. At the beginning of the school year, practitioners can ask, "What are your dreams and aspirations for your child?" and "How can we work together to accomplish these goals?"

School staff can be coached on constructive ways to approach home visits and conferences with families. Additionally, they need the opportunity, space, and time to reflect on their family engagement values and practices, which can be accomplished through professional development sessions that allow them to reflect on their practices and their beliefs about the families they work with.

- **Offer family engagement courses to educators during pre-service.** Pre-service teacher programs need to include family engagement courses to expose teachers in training to research that illustrates family engagement's importance and relevance (like the research presented in this book) and to introduce best practices for working with families. Additionally, pre-service teachers should be given opportunities to work with families. They should, for example, practice having conversations with families, introducing themselves, and discussing families' hopes and dreams for their children.

Recommendation 6: Extend networks and partnerships.

- **Create opportunities for parent and family leadership.** Family engagement practices can empower parents and develop their leadership skills. Provide opportunities for family members to use those skills by creating parent and family councils, task forces and committees, parent-teacher associations, and parent and family advisory boards. Be sure those groups are representative of the population the school serves. In other words, recruitment efforts need to include even the "hard to reach" families, which is why having strong relationships with families is essential. Partner with parents to recruit other parents for leadership roles and opportunities. After all, a parent-to-parent relationship is a great source of support.

- **Use community organizing efforts to share power with families.** Leaders in community-based organizations also need to share power with families, especially when they're organizing and strategizing for social change. Those leaders, as well as members of the organizations, should invest in relational trust (i.e., getting to know community members), learn local histories, and understand the community's most pressing needs by talking to families and community members of all backgrounds.

- **Leverage outside resources.** Collaborate with local organizations and public officials to bring additional funds, opportunities, and supports into schools and communities. For example, partner with local food banks to provide meals for families, or community health clinics to provide annual vision checks for students. Additionally, it is important that this be a collaborative, power-sharing process with both families and stakeholders. Instead of gathering resources *for* families, work *with* families to develop the relationships and connections they need to achieve their goals. This applies to school-based initiatives and community-based organizations. For example, service planning committees should include parent leaders to advocate for services for which fellow parents have expressed a pressing need.

Final Considerations

Now that we know what we know about family engagement, what are we going to do about it? What works is a system, or infrastructure, of connection, support, and leadership development centered on student and family well-being. Young children thrive in pre-K programs in which their teachers collaborate with their families to promote their development. Parents can create a stimulating home learning environment when teachers explain what their children are learning and doing in class and share interactive strategies that families can use.

Those practices have ripple effects. Teachers feel more supported and informed when parents explain their children's interests and challenges. Guidance counselors, social workers, special education teachers, and reading specialists can provide vital support to both families and teachers. Community organizations that offer childcare, after-school, and summer enrichment programs allow parents to work and children to expand their horizons. When school districts offer community education programs, health clinics, recreation centers, and GED classes, the whole community benefits. When community organizations offer parent leadership training, the community's culture becomes more vibrant, equitable, and effective for all families. In short: EVERYONE WINS!

The traditional picture of family engagement shows a parent, a teacher, and a student in a school building. But family engagement is much more than that. Think of it as a rocket launch! Just as engineers, mathematicians, mechanics, and ground crews work together to launch a rocket, so, too, do families, educators, support staff, administrators, and community organizations work together to launch children's success.

The research presented in this book demonstrates the potential, value, and necessity of investing in family engagement work. We hope it will convince policy-makers, public officials, program developers, administrators, community organizers, and educators that engaging families is an essential, even foundational strategy for creating the effective, equity-driven schools that all our children deserve. Such schools are wonderful places to learn and to work— and to connect, heal, and liberate.

We also hope that the big stories, major findings, and specific recommendations that emerge from the research will guide new and robust initiatives to transform the dispositions and mindsets of teachers and administrators; create welcoming, inclusive cultures in schools; and build equitable partnerships among families, school staff, and community organizations.

STUDY SUMMARIES

This section contains one-page summaries of the recent and time-honored studies we highlighted and described in Chapters 1–4 of this book.

STUDY SUMMARIES BY TYPE

Qualitative		page
Literature Review	Jensen & Minke (2017)	136
	Van Voorhis et al. (2013)	152
Report based on interviews, surveys, and/ or site visits	Ascher & Maguire (2007)	119
	Baker et al. (2016)	120
	Barbour et al. (2018)	121
	Caspe & Lopez (2018)	125
	Cuevas (2019)	126
	Geller et al. (2019)	128
	McKnight et al. (2017)	142
	Quiñones & Marquez Kiyama (2014)	146
	TalkingPoints (2021)	151
	Venkateswaran et al. (2018)	153
Descriptive Case Study	Baxter & Toe (2021)	122
	Flores & Kyere (2020)	127
	Ishimaru (2019)	134
	Sanders (2014)	149
	Warren & Mapp (2011)	154
	Warren, Mapp, & Kuttner (2015)	155
Ethnography	Ginwright (2016, 2018)	129
	Hong (2011)	131
	Hong (2019)	132
Portraiture	Lawrence-Lightfoot (2003)	139

Quantitative		page
Correlational	Allensworth, Ponisciak, & Mazzeo (2009)	117
	Bryk et al. (2010)	124
	Hayakawa et al. (2013)	130
	MacIver et al. (2015)	141
	Reynolds & Clements (2005)	148
Experimental	Angrist et al. (2020)	118
	Kraft & Dougherty (2013)	137
	Kraft & Rogers (2015)	138
Quasi-Experimental	Piccinino et al. (2020)	145
	Welch (2018)	156

Mixed-Method	page
Bryk & Schneider (2002)	123
Humphrey & Squires (2011)	133
Ishimaru (2020)	135
Learning Heroes (2018)	140
McLaughlin, Fehrer, & Leos-Urbel (2020)	143
Mediratta, Shah, & McAlister (2009)	144
Rangel, Shoji, & Gamoran (2020)	147
Sheldon & Jung (2018)	150

The Schools Teachers Leave:
Teacher Mobility in Chicago Public Schools

Elaine Allensworth, Stephen Ponisciak, and Christopher Mazzeo • 2009

SUMMARY: This quantitative study examines the factors that affect high teacher mobility in Chicago Public Schools (CPS), including teacher and student backgrounds, school structure, and workplace conditions. Three factors are most significant: Teachers' relationships with parents, students' behavior, and a strong sense of collaboration among teachers and the principal.

BACKGROUND: Fewer than half of new Chicago teachers stay in their elementary or high school for more than four years. This disrupts school functioning and undermines efforts to build a high-performing team of teachers and administrators. Other problems include shortages in key subjects, loss of experienced teachers, not enough time to recruit new teachers, and lower student success.

DESIGN OF STUDY: This study identifies school conditions that promote teacher retention or trigger departures, including leadership, the learning climate, and teachers' relationships with the principal, parents, and colleagues. The researchers used teachers' personnel records, student and school records, and surveys of almost 35,000 teachers in over 650 schools.

FINDINGS: Schools with high numbers of low-income, African American students have lower stability rates than schools serving other students. Two working conditions account for most of the differences in stability rates: teachers' relationships with parents and teachers' perceptions of students' behavior. Schools that have inclusive leadership and a strong sense of collaboration retain teachers; schools where colleagues resist schoolwide improvement efforts lose teachers.

In elementary schools, how teachers see parents as partners is strongly related to their decisions to remain. Even in low-income schools, teachers are much more likely to remain where most parents pick up report cards, attend parent-teacher conferences and school events, volunteer to help, and raise funds for the school. In high schools, teachers tend to leave when rates of student disciplinary problems are high. However, at both elementary and high schools, teachers are more likely to remain if there are high levels of trust with parents. In high-trust schools, teachers feel that parents respect them and support their work.

CONCLUSIONS: The factors that most strongly predict teacher stability reflect the control teachers have over their work environment, including conditions that limit their ability to do their jobs. Teachers are more likely to stay in schools where they feel that they have influence over school decisions, supportive principals and cooperative colleagues, and families who trust, respect, and support them. These parent-teacher interactions are shaped not only by parents but also by the ways the school communicates with parents and offers opportunities for parent involvement.

CONSIDERATIONS FOR THE FIELD: These findings point the way for measures that can improve conditions for teachers and students and promote collaboration and trust. This includes professional development for administrators in collaborative management and shared decision-making, for teachers in positive classroom disciplinary strategies, and for school staff in building trusting relationships with families.

Stemming Learning Loss During the Pandemic: A Rapid Randomized Trial of a Low-Tech Intervention in Botswana

Noam Angrist, Peter Bergman, Caton Brewster, and Moitshepi Matsheng • 2020

SUMMARY: This rapid randomized trial, conducted in Botswana during the COVID-19 pandemic, found that low-cost interventions of text messages and phone calls to primary school parents reduced innumeracy and boosted parent engagement.

BACKGROUND: In March 2020, a few days before nationwide school closures were officially announced, the research team leveraged school-based staff from the NGO Young 1ove to collect 7,550 phone numbers from Botswana primary schools. All schools sampled hosted active Teaching at the Right Level (TaRL) programming, an initiative that had reached 15 percent of Botswana primary schools at the time of the study and whose programming has led to marked improvements in literacy and numeracy for participating students.

DESIGN OF STUDY: Of the phone numbers collected, 4,550 households agreed to participate in the study. These families were randomized into three groups of equal size: a control group that received no intervention, a treatment arm that received weekly SMS messages only, and a treatment arm that received weekly SMS messages followed by a direct phone call. At the beginning of each week, the first intervention with text messages sent participants a one-way SMS with several simple math problems. Those receiving the second intervention with a text and phone call treatment participated in a 15–20 minute phone call with their facilitator that provided support, motivation, and accountability.

FINDINGS: Based on the first wave of results, students in the treatment groups made marked improvements in numeracy. More numeracy gains were made by students in the lower levels than in higher levels. Based on these findings, these low-tech interventions have the potential to close learning gaps between higher- and lower-performing students, even without pre-existing relationships with their facilitators. Overall, both interventions yielded high engagement among both students and their parents.

CONCLUSIONS: This study is one of the first of its kind to provide experiential results on minimizing the negative learning impacts of COVID-19, with encouraging results for higher rates of learning and increased engagement through low-cost, scalable programming.

CONSIDERATIONS FOR THE FIELD: The low-cost, low-tech interventions evaluated in this study are scalable across contexts, while still holding a great deal of potential for personalization from the local to national level. While these types of interventions are not the be-all end-all of parent engagement, they are affordable, easy-to-roll-out programs to mitigate learning loss and maintain ties with students and families during school-closure shocks.

Beating the Odds: How Thirteen NYC Schools Bring Low-Performing Ninth Graders to Timely Graduation and College Enrollment

Carol Ascher and Cindy Maguire • 2007

SUMMARY: What characterizes high performing high schools that serve low-income students? This qualitative study examined 13 high schools in New York City with graduation rates 10 points or more above the district average. All served nearly 100 percent low-income students of color. Using a four-component framework and indicators, the authors identified effective practices that include extensive and close collaboration with families.

BACKGROUND: At the time of this study, New York City's four-year graduation rate was 57 percent. Yet some high schools were successful in bringing students with low academic skills and high needs to timely graduation and enrollment in college. This study focused on a small group of New York City high schools that, according to 2001 data, were "beating the odds." In these BTO schools, the student poverty rate was above the district average. The students were mostly Black or Hispanic and more likely to be over age for their grade.

DESIGN OF STUDY: The authors developed an interview protocol focused on four areas of practice seen as critical to academic success among low-performing students: Academic rigor, a network of timely supports, a culture of college access, and effective use of data. For each component, they developed a rubric laying out effective practices and levels of implementation. Based on interviews and observations, the rubric become a roadmap to how lower-performing schools could improve their practices, allowing the findings to be scaled up across the system.

FINDINGS: The BTO schools admitted ninth graders with low reading and math scores but produced four-year graduation rates 10 points above the district average. Thirty-five percent planned to attend the City University of New York, compared to 28.3 percent of students in comparison schools. The component with the strongest connection to families is the culture of college access. The BTO schools used a variety of practices to expose students and families to college: building relationships with a few public and private colleges, offering workshops on the college application and financial aid process, hosting visits from colleges, holding a Hispanic College Fair for undocumented students, and partnering with the city's College Now program.

CONCLUSIONS: This study makes clear that the success of BTO schools is not a matter of chance. The schools emerged because the principals and staff boosted prospects for success. Enabling all students to graduate in a timely manner and obtain post-secondary education should not depend on a few heroic educators. Instead, high schools need resources, greater control over enrollment, recognition for their success, and a stronger system of district support and accountability

CONSIDERATIONS FOR THE FIELD: Helping families stay engaged through high school is critical to students' staying in school, taking more challenging classes, graduating on time, and going on to postsecondary programs. Some of the changes to standard practice these 13 schools made include rigorous academics, collaboration with community resources to provide extra support for students and families, strong guidance counseling, a student advisory system, and short-term pull-outs for extra academic support.

Identifying Barriers: Creating Solutions to Improve Family Engagement

Timberly L. Baker, Jillian Wise, Gwendolyn Kelley, and Russell J. Skiba • 2016

SUMMARY: This study examines the barriers to parents to family involvement and the solutions that could increase family engagement.

BACKGROUND: The authors present data collected through focus groups in six schools in a Midwestern state to examine how schools can move from parent involvement to parent engagement. The authors define parent involvement as "the focus on parents being present in the schools" while parent engagement is the "intentional efforts by the school to recognize and respond to parents' voices and to help school staff to better understand how to address barriers that parents have identified" (p.163).

DESIGN OF THE STUDY: The study focused on the following research questions: (1) What are the barriers or limitations to families attending school events?; and (2) What can be done differently to increase family involvement? Parents and staff from six different schools participated in 20 focus groups.

FINDINGS: Findings identified five themes across both groups (parents and staff): (1) Providing opportunities for involvement, taking constraints into consideration; (2) improving communication between parents and schools; (3) finding ways to welcome families into the building; (4) addressing parents' time conflicts; and (5) developing strategies to move from involvement to engagement.

Two themes were identified by staff:

1. **Overcoming Negative School Experiences:** Staff identified parents' past school experiences as possible barriers to their involvement in schools.

2. **Breaking Down Barriers to Access:** Staff also identified access to transportation and sustaining involvement from single family homes and foster homes. Staff also identified background checks for volunteers and the cost of involvement as other major barriers.

CONCLUSIONS: The authors concluded that "schools should embrace a more expansive view of parent engagement which includes multiple constructions of how parents are involved… moving from parent presence to engagement may require a profound attitude shift that focuses on the strengths and resources that families can bring to their child's education (Peña, 2000) and intentional and consistent attention to addressing barriers with connected solutions" (p.180).

CONSIDERATIONS FOR THE FIELD: This study provides a critical look at how schools can reframe parent involvement into a framework that encourages parent engagement. By providing data from both school staff and parents, this study provides a more holistic look at how each group understands the barriers and possible solutions needed to improve family involvement/ engagement in schools.

Parental Engagement Fund Study

Laura Barbour, Naomi Eisenstadt, Janet Goodall, Fiona Jelley, and Kathy Sylva • 2018

SUMMARY: This qualitative study examined five early intervention programs that engage low-income families in strengthening home learning. The researchers offered support for the programs to design and conduct their own evaluation. The process yielded rich practice information on what works to recruit and engage families, and to sustain that engagement.

BACKGROUND: The Sutton Trust aims to address inequality in children's early learning and develop effective family engagement practice in the UK. This study, funded by the Trust and conducted by the Parent Engagement Fund (PEF), compares five interventions to change parents' home learning practices during their children's early years. The study piloted a new model to develop the capacity of the programs to design, deliver, and evaluate their own work.

DESIGN OF STUDY: PEF selected five nonprofit organizations that were working with parents and showed "persistent curiosity" about their impact on parents and children. Four programs work directly with parents; the fifth trains school staff to engage parents in enriching the home learning environment. PEF provided three forms of support: funding to deliver a program to a target group, a "critical friend" to coach each group in evaluation process, and practical support, such as creating a network to share ideas and results. A total of 1,329 families took part.

FINDINGS: The findings fell into four categories.

1. Recruiting and keeping families
2. Engaging families
3. Pros and cons of various delivery models
4. Promoting active engagement and an improved home learning environment

Educators said the experience helped them gain greater understanding of the means and value of engaging parents. This, in turn, strengthened their confidence and capacity to support that engagement. It was gratifying to observe parents and children interacting happily around learning and the greater ease parents had communicating with teachers.

CONCLUSIONS: Establishing trust and collaboration between parents and teachers at the outset is essential to later success. It was shown that trying new methods to engage families is an effective and gratifying form of professional development and capacity-building, builds teacher buy-in, and can lead to lasting changes in their practice.

Combining direct support to families in their home environment with training teachers to engage families as part of the learning process in early childhood settings, appears to be more effective than one approach or the other. Parents are more likely to use what they learn with their children when they have opportunities to see how an activity is done and then practice it. In addition, parents benefit from learning from each other, creating new activities, and sharing strategies.

CONSIDERATIONS FOR THE FIELD: The goal of this study is to reduce or eliminate learning gaps between low-income and middle-class children. The findings are useful for program planning, professional development, indicators of program quality, and sharing with family networks.

Teachers' Use of Social Media for Family Engagement

Gillian Baxter and Dianne Toe • 2021

SUMMARY: This Critical Participatory Action Research (CPAR) study examined Australian primary school leaders' efforts to enhance family engagement in their children's learning through classroom teachers' use of social media. The three schools are in a culturally diverse community. Careful, constant actions to modify social media posts yielded significant changes in practices, moving from rote involvement in schooling to active family engagement in learning.

BACKGROUND: Social media platforms offer schools opportunities to enhance communication with families. Digital platforms allow teachers to upload instructional materials that allow students, families, and teachers to interact when and where they choose. While social media can connect families to their children's learning, its effectiveness needs more study. CPAR focused on examining local practices through participants' perspectives.

DESIGN OF STUDY: The participants formed a Family School Partnership Advisory Group with a team of teachers from each school: A Cluster Engagement in Learning Leader (CELL) coordinated the work across the entire project. Each principal selected one grade to be the focus.

Participating families completed an online survey at the start of the project and midway. The group used the survey data to reflect on their social media practices. Data included student work samples and images of students engaged in school activities and discussions.

Each school selected a different social media platform but used the same five-step CPAR process: 1) Gathering history about the use of social media; 2) Sharing the history in light of the survey data and samples of recent posts; 3) Considering their practice using a local context lens; 4) Transforming the practice, using the information and reflection so far; 5) Documenting and monitoring to identify opportunities, measure success, and plan next steps.

FINDINGS: Early social media posts to families were mostly descriptions and images of children's classroom learning, limiting them to the classroom context. After noting this limitation, school leaders collaborated with teachers and students to highlight learning connections across home and community contexts. In two schools, teachers revised social media posts so that families could talk with their children about learning, contributing their own knowledge and experiences. At the third school, teachers enhanced students' agency in developing posts so they could discuss their learning more effectively with their families.

CONCLUSIONS: While using different approaches, each school sought to reframe children's learning from being school-centric to occurring across home, community, and school contexts. The schools' actions to modify social media posts showed significant changes, producing higher levels of family engagement.

CONSIDERATIONS FOR THE FIELD: Using a well-designed process of critical inquiry focused on teacher and school practice of family engagement can yield insights, improve practice, and create more authentic partnerships among school leaders, teachers, students, and families.

Trust in Schools: A Core Resource for Improvement

Anthony S. Bryk and Barbara Schneider • 2002

SUMMARY: This rigorous, long-term study of elementary schools in Chicago found that the presence of relational trust significantly increased the likelihood of improved student achievement. Schools are social enterprises, and their success depends on a high level of cooperation among teachers, parents, and educators.

BACKGROUND: Too often, the lack of parent-teacher trust, often aggravated by differences of race and class, makes genuine dialogue difficult. The misunderstandings that result tend to reinforce existing biases. This study explores how trust is a key factor in improving the academic success of disadvantaged urban schools.

DESIGN OF STUDY: Using research on social trust, the authors developed a concept they call "relational trust." In a social setting like a school, the quality of social exchanges has enormous significance. Based on this research and their observations in schools, Bryk and Schneider identified four "considerations" that underlie trust: respect, competence, personal regard for others, and integrity. Relational trust deepens when we feel that others care about us, know what they're doing, keep their word, and will "go to bat" for us.

This study drew on data from case studies and observations of 12 Chicago elementary schools, analysis of data on 400 elementary schools, and two citywide teacher surveys three years apart, using three scales: teacher-parent trust, teacher-teacher trust, and teacher-principal trust. It compared levels of trust among the 100 top achieving schools with those in the bottom 100 and case studies of three elementary schools, two with low trust and one with a high level of trust.

FINDINGS: In general, higher levels of trust in schools predicted higher student performance, and lower levels predicted lower student performance. When the researchers compared schools' productivity, another interesting pattern emerged: Schools with higher levels of trust were much more likely to improve over time.

CONCLUSIONS: Trust is foundational to the healthy, effective functioning of a school and cannot be achieved simply through a workshop or sensitivity training, although all can be helpful. Rather, relational trust is forged in daily social exchanges. Through their actions, members of a school community demonstrate commitment to each other and to the purpose of the school.

CONSIDERATIONS FOR THE FIELD: Teachers receive little training in how to work with parents and community members. Effective urban schools need to recruit and retain teachers who know their students well, have empathy and understanding of the parents' situations, and have interpersonal skills needed to engage their students' families. Parents must be able to talk with teachers and have a say in how their children are treated. Teachers need to voice their concerns to administrators and feel they will be considered. Administrators need to feel that faculty cares about the functioning of the school. As John Dewey famously said, a school should be more like a family than a factory.

Organizing Schools for Improvement

Anthony S. Bryk, Penny B. Sebring, Elaine Allensworth, Stuart Luppescu, and John Q. Easton • 2010

SUMMARY: This landmark quantitative study compared schools in Chicago that made substantial improvement with similar schools that had stagnated or declined. The authors found five "essential supports" that led to school improvement. Schools that had "strong ties to families and the community" were four times more likely to make significant gains in reading and math.

BACKGROUND: Using the Consortium on Chicago School Research's deep database, the researchers identified five essential supports for school improvement present in schools that made major gains in reading and math, but had been absent or weak in schools that had not improved.

DESIGN OF STUDY: The researchers used complex statistical modeling to analyze 15 years of data from 395 public elementary schools (K–8) collected by the Consortium using surveys, field studies, school reports, and student test scores. Then they studied how the five essential supports interacted to reinforce each other to create pathways for advancing student achievement.

FINDINGS: The five essential supports are: a coherent instructional guidance system, professional capacity, strong parent-community-school ties, a student-centered learning climate, and leadership as a driver for change. The indicators for parent-school-community ties are teachers' ties to the community, teacher outreach to parents, parent involvement, and relational trust. Schools with strong indicators on most supports were 10 times more likely to improve than schools with weak supports. Sustained weakness in any one support undermined improvement; those schools rarely improved.

CONCLUSIONS: School improvement is like baking a cake. All ingredients are needed or it flops. Local school leadership is the catalyst for change. Principals organize and allocate the resources needed to create conditions for improvement. Trusting relationships are the soil in which everything takes root. Without them, it's nearly impossible to strengthen parent-community ties, build professional capacity, and enable a student-centered learning climate.

Truly disadvantaged school communities present unique challenges. Improving schools were found in all kinds of neighborhoods, but "stagnating schools" were mainly in poor, racially isolated African American areas. The social capital of a neighborhood where residents have a history of working together is a significant resource for improving its school. In contrast, the absence of social capital made it more likely that a troubled school would continue to stagnate.

All five essential supports are critical for school improvement. They must be especially strong for significant improvement in student learning to occur in disadvantaged communities.

CONSIDERATIONS FOR THE FIELD: This study offers some of the most convincing evidence we have that engaging families in deep and meaningful ways is a core strategy for school improvement. It is not something that can be done later, or in isolation from other efforts to advance student learning. It is NOT optional. The indicators of "close ties with parents and communities" deserve our attention. They are both deeper and broader than indicators traditionally used in our field.

Preparing the Next Generation of Librarians for Family and Community Engagement

Margaret Caspe and M. Elena Lopez • 2018

SUMMARY: To be successful at their jobs, librarians must engage and partner with families and communities. This qualitative study identifies the competencies and supports needed by librarians to successfully engage with families and communities.

BACKGROUND: In this article, Caspe and Lopez link the importance of family and community engagement to the role of libraries and librarians. Libraries are in a unique position to carry out family and community engagement work; they have access to different populations, are hubs for social services, and offer access to resources. Libraries are also spaces families visit to learn new ways to support student learning and development and connect with other families and community members. "Family engagement in libraries can be broadly defined as the process by which families and libraries join together to share the responsibility of supporting children's learning and development, from birth through adulthood" (p. 159).

DESIGN OF THE STUDY: To investigate what librarians should be taught about the importance of meaningful family and community engagement, the authors conducted interviews with 11 library educators at top schools of information and library sciences in the United States. Participants were asked questions about the knowledge, skills, and dispositions new librarians should have to successfully work with families and communities. They were also asked about current training for librarians and the extent to which their education covered family and community engagement topics, and to reflect on the best teaching methods, or pedagogy, used to discuss family and community engagement topics with future librarians.

FINDINGS: Caspe and Lopez presented their findings in two categories: (1) the knowledge, skills, and dispositions necessary for librarians, current and future, to develop to meaningfully engage with families and communities; and (2) the best pedagogical approaches to promote these competencies.

The three main goals to prepare librarians to meaningfully engage with families and communities are: (1) provide information to librarians about the families and communities they work with, (2) help librarians build relationships with families and communities, and (3) help librarians internalize the position that they are professionals who have the responsibility to help people. Librarians serve as advocates for the families and communities they work with.

CONCLUSIONS: This study makes clear the importance of family and community engagement in the work of libraries and librarians. If trained on family engagement competencies—understanding families and communities, relationship-building, and professionalism—librarians can be powerful advocates in communities.

CONSIDERATIONS FOR THE FIELD: This study draws attention to the importance of librarian training programs, calling on these programs to reevaluate how they train future librarians. Being that relationship-building and partnership with families and communities is of great importance, the study also serves as a call to both universities and community libraries to work together to improve how families and communities experience libraries.

"Con mucho sacrificio, we give them everything we can": The Strategic Sacrifices of Undocumented Latina/o Parents

Stephany Cuevas • 2019

SUMMARY: This qualitative study explores how undocumented Latinx parents engage in their children's post-secondary goals and aspirations. Undocumented parents make intentional day-to-day sacrifices for their children's educational attainment, often prioritizing their children's needs over their own basic needs. The findings indicate the importance of considering the impact of immigration status on Latinx parental engagement.

BACKGROUND: Cuevas explores how parents' undocumented immigration status shapes their engagement behaviors. The study is based on the experiences of 10 families—15 undocumented Latinx parents (10 mothers, 5 fathers)—who live in California. Primary data consisted of 30 in-depth semi-structured interviews in Spanish. Parents were asked about how they provided support to their children when they were in high school, how different life experiences impacted this support, and the challenges they faced.

FINDINGS: Undocumented parents intentionally engaged in behaviors that supported their children's post-secondary aspirations. Cuevas calls these behaviors *sacrificios*, or sacrifices, which often come at a very high personal cost. Day-to-day *sacrificios* include:

- Financially prioritizing children's needs
- Managing feelings of inferiority when engaging with schools
- Risking deportation and unemployment during daily tasks, such as driving their children to different curricular activities
- Managing limited time and risk losing jobs to attend school events

CONCLUSIONS: The study's findings illustrate how parents' undocumented immigration status impacts their engagement in their children's education, especially their higher education aspirations. In the process, undocumented Latinx parents often engage in behaviors that are traditionally conceived to belong to upper- and middle-class parents.

CONSIDERATIONS FOR THE FIELD: Considering our contemporary political climate, in which undocumented immigrants have become scapegoats for economic decline and are victims of nativist and racialized hate crimes, it is essential that we consider how parents' undocumented immigration status affects their engagement. How can their immigration status become a barrier to engagement? As Cuevas notes, "the consequences and limitations of parents' illegality not only shape their engagement with their children's post-secondary planning and success but how they live their everyday lives." This is a much-needed contribution to immigration and family engagement practice and research.

Advancing Equity-Based School Leadership: The Importance of Family–School Relationships

Osly J. Flores and Eric Kyere • 2020

SUMMARY: This interpretive qualitative inquiry presents the parent engagement stories of five social justice and equity-oriented urban public school principals. This study explores what it means to move productive parent engagement from rhetoric into action, particularly for historically marginalized students and families. The study offers best practice approaches on how educators can examine, frame, and direct parent engagement in their schools.

BACKGROUND: Prompted by a lack of the research on the intersection between parent involvement and school leadership from an equity standpoint, the authors focus this study on identifying best practice approaches by school leaders for parent engagement in schools. The study describes the practices of social justice leadership for parent engagement by exploring the *how*, *what*, and *why* of building positive relationships with parents. The study underscores the significance for social justice and equity-oriented school leaders in urban contexts of strong and trusting parent relationships.

DESIGN OF STUDY: The study is a secondary analysis of data from a larger study of how principals direct their leadership toward equitable practices that enhance learning for all students. The research method of narrative inquiry was used to collect the lived experiences of principals.

FINDINGS: The findings highlight the role that relationships with parents can contribute to effective parent-school engagement in ways that are culturally and contextually responsive and empower parents to support children's educational outcomes. The authors develop an equity-based parent engagement model of why and how the five school leaders built positive relationships with parents. The findings revealed that the school leaders practiced family/parent engagement from a social justice and equity standpoint by building trusting relationships, engaging in intentional self-refection and the resistance of deficit-thinking, and connecting the family engagement work to equity. The school leaders saw the outcomes of positive relationships with parents as the recognition from parents of their commitment to students, the support of their school success goals, the parents' trust of their leadership decision-making, and the greater opportunities for student success.

CONCLUSIONS: Trustful relationships with families and communities are key mechanisms by which school leaders can enact their practices to attend to the principles of democratic participation and the social justice needs of the families/communities they serve.

CONTRIBUTIONS: Few studies have captured the essence of how school leaders interpret the outcomes of positive relationship with parents. The model also contributes to the parent engagement literature by highlighting equity-minded school leaders' practice and the underlying value of parent/family engagement.

The Ripple Effect in Action: What Seven Parent Leadership Initiatives Learned from Participatory Evaluation

Joanna Geller, Jessamyn Luiz, Danielle Asher, Sara McAlister, Anne T. Henderson, Kate Gill Kressley, Wendy Perez, and Joy Sanzone, eds. • 2019

SUMMARY: In this qualitative study, seven parent leadership initiatives (PLIs) across the United States evaluated their work to assess impact, identify successful practices, and enhance effectiveness. Investment in family-strengthening and healing-centered engagement had a transformational impact on parent leaders and their families and communities.

BACKGROUND: In 2014, meetings among parent leadership initiatives, funders, researchers, and community organizations, found that initiatives to develop parent leadership had not been well documented or understood. Working with parent leaders, the authors developed and used an evaluation framework and appropriate metrics to study their work.

DESIGN OF STUDY: Partnering with Dialogues in Action, the researchers and parent leaders from the parent leadership organizations developed and applied an Indicators Framework to evaluate their work. Using an in-depth interview protocol with a purposeful, stratified sample of parent leaders, each group identified major themes and findings, and considered the implications for program improvement and innovation.

FINDINGS: The interviews showed that parent leaders moved from seeing themselves as just a parent or a worrier, to become change agents, role models, and the go-to person in their families and community. This transformation was the force behind significant policy wins made by these PLIs over the past few years. These include passing minimum wage increases, heading off deep budget cuts to services for children and families, and replacing "zero tolerance" school discipline policies with restorative justice programs.

The PLI teams identified five practices that led to these transformative impacts: Fostering families' well-being and building on their strengths; creating a community that feels like a safe, supportive family; creating a sense of positive identity and pride in one's culture; and empowering through skill- and knowledge-building.

CONCLUSIONS: Many evidence-based programs that focus on families produce short-term effects, but not durable change. This study concludes that longer-term investments in personal growth build power in ways that are essential to lasting, transformational change. A campaign may "win" new resources but not guarantee that the benefits will be fully and fairly implemented. There also must be a redistribution of power so that parent leaders have a voice in implementation and a role in holding officials accountable for results.

CONSIDERATIONS FOR THE FIELD: Most programs to engage families in improving children's outcomes offer knowledge, skills, and opportunities to practice them. This study suggests that such efforts would be more successful if they also created a "second family" that can strengthen families by affirming their contributions and personal value, connecting them to economic and social resources, building their capacity to support their children's learning and development, listening to their ideas, and developing their voices.

Hope and Healing in Urban Education:
How Urban Activists and Teachers Are Reclaiming Matters of the Heart

Shawn Ginwright • 2016

SUMMARY: Rooted in five case studies, this ethnographic study examined how "radical healing" can change distressed urban communities. Bringing young people together to heal from trauma, identify what they want their schools and communities to be like, and taking "imaginative action" to implement their vision leads to collective well-being.

BACKGROUND: This book illustrates how local leaders can change their communities "from the inside out," using radical healing that builds capacity to contribute to the common good. Developing personal well-being, community health, and broader social justice allows people to act for others "with hope, joy, and a sense of possibility." Ginwright distinguishes this approach from trauma-informed care because it addresses what causes trauma in the first place.

DESIGN OF STUDY: Ginwright first examined how community activists are using healing strategies to support young people. Then, through observation and analysis, he showed how a focus on healing can advance civic engagement, prompting disconnected young people to take action.

FINDINGS: In "Radically Healing Schools and Communities," Ginwright describes efforts in San Francisco Bay Area high schools to cool tensions, develop a vision for what could be better, and bring students, parents, teachers, and administrators together to discuss how to make it happen. A key strategy for success is forming a self-selected "critical inquiry group" of five to 10 teachers and administrators to reflect on the impact of racism and unconscious bias on student performance. and to discuss how to improve their teaching and healing practices.

The critical inquiry group worked to build more collaborative relationships among parents, teachers, and students. It used practices such as morning "community circles" to check in with students and set the tone for the day/week, documenting school values that are reflected in curriculum, teaching, assessment, and rules, and increasing student involvement via the student council. Once teachers established relationships of trust and respect with students, classroom culture began to change in positive ways.

CONCLUSIONS: Radical healing encourages teachers, activists, and young people to consider that the results that we seek depend on the quality of our relationships and the clarity of our consciousness. Successful policy change and interventions that create healing improve school climate and advance learning. Such interventions impact the interior condition of both adults and young people in the communities and schools we seek to transform.

CONSIDERATIONS FOR THE FIELD: Based on Ginwright's findings: 1) Recognize signs of collective and individual harm through healing circles that bring young people together with teachers and parents. 2) Define what well-being looks like in a school and engage in imaginative action. Visiting inspiring schools and community organizations is a good place to start. 3) Implement practices that facilitate healing by infusing a worldview of well-being, healing, and joy. We may need to start with healing ourselves; only then will we experience "successful" implementation.

The Longitudinal Process of Early Parent Involvement on Student Achievement: A Path Analysis

Momoko Hayakawa, Michelle M. Englund, Mallory N. Warner-Richter, and Arthur J. Reynolds • 2013

SUMMARY: This longitudinal study examined how early parent involvement in preschool has a lasting effect on student achievement from kindergarten through sixth grade. Nearly 1,000 low-income, mainly African American children and their mothers, took part for one or two years in the Chicago Child-Parent Center (CPC) program. Path analysis showed that early parent involvement directly influenced kindergarten achievement, which in turn influenced first grade student motivation. This process continued to produce better results through sixth grade.

BACKGROUND: Early in their lives, young children are optimistic, highly motivated, and positively inclined toward learning in school, traits that often decline in their later years. If that early receptivity can be carried forward, it is important to understand how to sustain it throughout children's academic careers. This study explores whether students' motivation influences parent involvement, which then fuels subsequent student motivation. Given the link between student motivation and academic achievement, does student motivation act as a mediating variable that can explain the persistent influence of early parent involvement on later achievement?

DESIGN OF STUDY: The study sample was taken from the Chicago Longitudinal Study of 1,539 racial minority children (93 percent African American, 7 percent Hispanic). Children in the intervention and comparison groups were matched on child and family characteristics, such as race/ethnicity, gender, and family risk factors, such as low income and single parenthood. The sample was evenly split between males and females.

FINDINGS: Findings strongly suggested that early parent involvement promoted in the CPC program sets the stage for subsequent parent involvement, student motivation, and academic achievement throughout early and middle childhood. These findings confirmed the idea that motivation plays an integral role in the cycle of parent involvement and student achievement.

CONCLUSIONS: While some early interventions have produced initial gains, they failed to sustain increased achievement later in school. Findings from this study not only provide a potential solution to decreasing the early achievement gap, but more important, provide a mechanism through which the early effects of parent involvement and achievement can be carried forward through elementary school and beyond.

CONSIDERATIONS FOR THE FIELD: This is yet another important study showing the lasting impact of high-quality early childhood education programs that incorporate robust family engagement. Its unique contribution is revealing the pathways of effects that create the strong, positive outcomes for children's achievement. As suggested by several other studies, what counts is the quality and sustained continuation of involvement. Investment in well-designed programs yields lasting effects and long-term cost savings.

A Cord of Three Strands: A New Approach to Parent Engagement in Schools

Soo Hong • 2011

SUMMARY: This two-year ethnographic study is an analysis of the evolution of one model of parent engagement developed by the Logan Square Neighborhood Association (LSNA), a community organization with deep ties to the Latino immigrant families on Chicago's Northwest Side. The study offers a three-part *ecology of parent engagement* to conceptualize and design successful parent engagement strategies, practices, and initiatives.

BACKGROUND: Many techniques used by schools to engage parents are rooted in traditional notions of parent involvement where schools design activities and parents are asked to endorse and fall in line with the programs. Whether these activities involve classroom volunteering, fundraising activities, parent conferences or open houses, in schools that have strained or distant relationships with families, attendance or participation is often low, leaving educators to often develop problematic and deficit-based reasons about the lack of involvement within the community. Through a focus on the LSNA and its work in one school, this study was designed to provide a rich, in-depth discussion that joins theoretical concepts with the process necessary for change.

DESIGN OF THE STUDY: Hong developed a qualitative methodology for this project called *layered ethnography*. She structured the study as a multiyear ethnography, and over a four-year period developed relationships with community organizers, parents, and school staff in the Logan Square neighborhood. Hong conducted interviews with parents, attended training sessions and leadership workshops, visited classrooms and walked the school hallways, and met with organizers.

FINDINGS: Hong designed a framework called *the ecology of parent engagement:* a three-part model considering the multiple contexts, interactions, and experiences that shape parent engagement:

1. **Parent engagement as induction:** developing engagement and participation opportunities that are designed to introduce parents to school environments and practices.

2. **Parent engagement as integration:** highlighting the ways engagement strategies can connect parents to other individuals in the school.

3. **Parent engagement as investment:** envisioning parent engagement in ways that build parents as leaders and active decision-makers within schools.

CONCLUSION: Hong warns readers not to view the elements of induction, integration, and investment as independent or sequential processes, but to see the power of the model in its recognition that the three processes are interactive, connected, and developmental.

CONSIDERATION FOR THE FIELD: This book presents an analysis of the issues that many schools face as well as effective practices in promoting meaningful change. This book offers current and future practitioners concrete ideas in working with families and communities.

Natural Allies: Hope and Possibility in Teacher-Family Partnerships

Soo Hong • 2019

SUMMARY: This ethnographic study examines the motivations and experiences of five teachers in Boston and Washington, D.C., who create meaningful and productive relationships and partnerships with students' families. The portraits of teachers and their experiences with students' families demonstrate how a commitment to cultivating and maintaining meaningful relationships with families and community should be a central part of educators' practices. The study provides insights on how the dynamics of race, class, culture, and family history with schools shape the interactions and potential for relationships between families and educators.

BACKGROUND: Hong examined the motivations and experiences of five urban teachers committed to partnership with families. Hong studied how teacher practices with families are shaped by their beliefs about families and communities, seeking to understand what teachers must do to cultivate such relationships with trust, care, and respect.

DESIGN OF STUDY: Hong used the qualitative methodology of portraiture to conduct her three-year ethnographic study. Key to her study was the selection of five teachers who developed and strengthened their ability to work with parents. The teachers reflected: 1) a long-term commitment and proven track record of success in engaging families and communities; 2) engagement with low-income urban communities typically viewed as "hard to reach;" and 3) diversity of age, years of experience, and race/ethnicity. Teachers also represented a range of pathways into the profession and taught in elementary and middle school classrooms, working with both native speakers and emergent bilinguals.

FINDINGS: The findings challenged the longstanding depiction of families and educators as "natural enemies," showing how through intentional practice grounded in trust and ongoing communication, families and educators can become natural allies instead. Hong argues that schools should become "grounded institutions"—"schools that are rooted in and reflect the full lives and experiences of students' families and communities" (p.160). To move beyond superficial interactions into more meaningful commitments to families, this study found teachers must develop a sense of trust and shared purpose.

CONCLUSIONS: This study illuminates the importance of teacher competency in family and community engagement as a fundamental element of high-quality teaching. The study offers new ideas on family engagement grounded in an analysis of the deep contours of the parent-teacher relationship.

CONSIDERATIONS FOR THE FIELD: This study offers a practice-based model to guide conversations and reforms necessary in family and community engagement. As school systems grapple with policies to drive and shape effective family and community engagement practice and capacity building, this study is an effective guide in establishing a strategic vision and plan.

Achievement for All National Evaluation: Final Report

Neil Humphrey and Garry Squires • 2011

SUMMARY: This mixed method study evaluated the *Achievement for All* (AfA) program in the United Kingdom, aimed at improving opportunities for students with special educational needs and disabilities (SEND). Over two years, 454 schools piloted the program, which included "structured conversations with parents," realizing significant gains in academic outcomes.

BACKGROUND: In the UK, "special educational needs" is defined broadly to include students from vulnerable groups, such as those whose first language is not English, are in foster care, or are eligible for free school meals. The 454 schools that participated received funding from the Department for Education for two years (2009–2011). AfA has three main strands: 1) Assessment, tracking and intervention; 2) Structured conversations with parents for an hour three times a year; and 3) "Wider outcomes" (attendance, behavior, and relationships).

DESIGN OF STUDY: Humphrey and Squires posed two main questions: What is the impact of AfA on SEND students? And what processes and practices are most effective in improving outcomes? They used quantitative analysis of attendance and academic progress data in AfA and comparison schools, teacher and parent surveys, interviews and focus groups, observations, case studies, and school documentation. They tracked changes over three years, from the year before implementation through pilot completion.

FINDINGS: The program narrowed the achievement gap between students with and without SEND. AfA schools saw marked improvements in English and Math scores compared to the national average for SEND students and even for all non-SEND students. "Wider outcomes" in non-academic areas such as confidence, behavior, and social relations, also significantly improved. Structured Conversations with Parents was the most successful strand, or as one school declared, "an absolute roaring success" (p. 58). Teachers deeply appreciated what they learned about their students from talking with parents. This component accounted for 43 percent of the variance in scores at the end of the pilot, making it central to student success (p. 60).

CONCLUSIONS: Anticipating that schools might water down the program, the authors strongly cautioned that the structured conversations with parents be fully supported and faithful to the original guidance. They also emphasized the role of parents in generating positive outcomes for SEND students, and "the need to view 'education' as encapsulating school and home, and the relationship between them" (p. 115).

CONSIDERATIONS FOR THE FIELD: This study gives ample evidence that close parent-teacher collaboration is a critical component of success in a program to improve outcomes for all students. Especially for students with special needs, positive relationships and welcoming school culture are integral to success. Individual student profiles illustrate how well students responded when teachers collaborated closely with their parents and used the information gained to meet their needs.

From Family Engagement to Equitable Collaboration

Ann M. Ishimaru • 2019

SUMMARY: This qualitative study used an equity-based framework to examine cross-sector collaboration initiatives to engage families and communities in their children's education.

BACKGROUND: This nested, comparative qualitative case study examines three initiatives within the Pathways Project, "a cross-sector collaborative initiative comprised of education, community, health, and other organizational partners located in a region of concentrated suburban poverty in a Western region of the United States" (p. 357). The three initiatives, two school-based and one neighborhood-based, were identified by the Pathways Project for their leadership in parent engagement, and they received funding and support to improve their programming.

DESIGN OF STUDY: Researchers conducted interviews and focus groups with program leaders and providers, district and school leaders, teachers, parents, and family support staff, collected 115 hours of observations at various meetings and events, and compiled extensive documentation. Analysis included multiple rounds of coding, sharing initial findings with sites and incorporating feedback, constructing case studies, and applying the dimensions of the conceptual framework.

FINDINGS: The three sites nested within the Pathways Project were working to improve equitable engagement practices through parent/family capacity-building, parent-school and parent-parent relationship-building, and systemic change and capacity-building. While their practices were still rooted in traditional involvement approaches that did not challenge power asymmetries between families and schools, the organizations initiated promising equitable strategies that focused on building relationships, parent capacities, and systemic capacities.

CONCLUSIONS: The study highlights the promises and limitations of efforts to foster more equitable relationships between schools, families, and communities in the context of cross-sector collaboration initiatives. The findings suggest policy implications for engaging in collaborative strategies that are jointly crafted by all stakeholders—education professionals, community leaders, and nondominant families alike. Ishimaru closes by inviting future research that explores "how we move from promising, but fragmented, schoolcentric strategies to integrated and systemic approaches that prioritize nondominant family and community goals and influence in pursuit of equity-based transformation and educational justice" (p. 380).

CONSIDERATIONS FOR THE FIELD: By drawing the focus away from traditionally individualistic, deficit-based efforts, the study hones in on galvanizing families as equal partners in power with schools. It highlights how cross-sector collaborations are susceptible to the trappings of top-down initiatives that push nondominant families out.

Just Schools: Building Equitable Collaborations With Families and Communities

Ann M. Ishimaru • 2020

SUMMARY: In *Just Schools*, Ann Ishimaru brings together research, theory, and practice to construct a road map to equitable collaboration with families and communities for educational justice. Ishimaru explores the ways in which systemic racial inequities play out in schools and provides guidelines for educators and community members to approach their work critically, shift power imbalances between schools and communities, and build solidarity for sustainable change.

BACKGROUND: *Just Schools* examines the complex intersecting dynamics that feed into common policies and best practices, particularly along lines of race, class, language, power, and privilege.

Ishimaru approaches this entanglement through a lens of equitable collaboration, which builds on critical race theory, community organizing, and sociocultural learning theories.

DESIGN OF STUDY: This book shares methods and evidence from empirical studies over the past decade, including qualitative, mixed method, and critical participatory action research.

FINDINGS: Throughout the chapters, the book analyzed how dynamics between nondominant communities and educational institutions play out at systemic, organizational, and individual levels. Dr. Ishimaru lays out her framework for navigating these interactions equitably through four inquiry-driven and ongoing principles: 1) Begin with family and community priorities, interests, concerns, knowledge and resources; 2) Transform power; 3) Build reciprocity and agency; 4) Undertake change as collective inquiry (p. 2). Rather than one-time goals to achieve or check off for completion, these guidelines are "starting places, strands of DNA for growing our practices and expanding our collective capacity" (p. 162). *Just Schools* includes several case studies that illustrate the ways in which these guidelines play out in different contexts, including the imperfections and mistakes that come with the territory.

CONCLUSION: Equitable collaboration with families and communities is not about checking boxes for completion or making it to a predetermined destination. It's about continuous work and inquiry to build an education experience that is in and of its community—every effort is unique and escapes the constraints of scalability. Dr. Ishimaru encourages solidarity and creation in these efforts by reminding readers to reject the binaries of an either/or mentality. Instead, embrace both/and. This continuous process of building solidarity with nondominant families and communities is essential to not only imagine systems and practices of true educational justice, but to build the collective capacity to make it real.

CONSIDERATIONS FOR THE FIELD: Dr. Ishimaru lays out the guidelines for equitable collaboration that tap into the uncertainty and opportunity of creation when enacting systemic change—each effort must begin with and be unique to its families and communities, which means that no successful, sustainable process is truly scalable. *Just Schools* ushers in the next evolution of the family and community engagement field by pushing past school-centric best practices and opening the imagination for collaborative, transformative change that reaches beyond education.

Engaging Families at the Secondary Level: An Underused Resource for Student Success

Krista L. Jensen and Kathleen M. Minke • 2017

SUMMARY: In this study, Jensen and Minke conduct a literature review of parent engagement research that focuses on the importance of engagement at the secondary level as it relates to positive outcomes for academic achievement, high school completion rates, and social-emotional functioning.

BACKGROUND: The article highlights the gaps in literature to address the notions that there are benefits and risks to parent engagement for older students and the expectations that high schools engage parents without as much research to inform practices.

DESIGN OF STUDY: Using online primary search databases, Jensen and Minke searched for studies that "included combinations of the following terms: parent involvement, parent engagement, parent participation, high school, secondary school, elementary school, academic/educational outcomes, high school completion, school dropout, and social/emotional outcomes" (p. 168).

FINDINGS: While the types of behaviors are different from those traditionally performed at the elementary level, parent engagement maintains a positive relationship with academic achievement through high school. Parents' decisions to become engaged are motivated by role construction and self-efficacy, or their beliefs about what responsibilities they have towards their child's education and whether their actions have a positive influence on outcomes. Notably, parents are more likely to engage in education when they feel they are welcomed and desired to do so.

CONCLUSION: This literature review compiles evidence that parent engagement is a significant factor in secondary education, as it influences academic achievement, graduation rates, and social/emotional outcomes. There is much research to be done at the secondary level, and "as we develop our understanding of adolescents' perceptions of and preferences for parent engagement and the roles that variables such as parent–adolescent relationship quality, adolescents' invitations for engagement, and family resources play in predicting parent engagement, we will be better positioned to produce positive outcomes for all students" (p. 185).

CONSIDERATIONS FOR THE FIELD: Despite some overemphasized popular examples of over-engagement (e.g., helicopter parents), parental engagement continues to have a positive relationship with student outcomes through secondary school. It takes different forms with adolescents than with younger children, such as more age-appropriate focuses on respecting and supporting autonomy, as well as navigating complex systems like high schools and colleges. School-family partnerships continue to be necessary components of education as students grow older, and secondary institutions can further increase equity by engaging all parents in planning their children's futures.

The Effects of Teacher-Family Communication on Student Engagement: Evidence From a Randomized Field Experiment

Matthew A. Kraft & Shaun M. Dougherty • 2013

SUMMARY: This randomized field experiment evaluated the relationship between teacher communication with parents and students and student engagement. Assigning a group of sixth- and ninth-grade students who attended a mandated summer school program to receive a daily phone call home and a text/written message from teachers, the authors examined the causal relationship between teacher-parent communication, teacher-student communication, and student outcomes.

BACKGROUND: To show a causal relationship between teacher communication with families and students and student engagement, Kraft and Dougherty conducted a randomized field experiment during the 2010 summer academy at the MATCH Charter Public Middle School and High School in Boston, Massachusetts. MATCH predominantly serves low-income students of color. All students in the treatment group were assigned to receive one phone call home per day for one week from either their fiction or nonfiction teacher and a text/written messages from their mathematics teachers. Teachers were given a common protocol to follow. The protocol asked teachers to communicate positive, neutral, or negative information as they saw fit but asked them to end the communication affirming that the student could be successful and offer one specific way the student could maintain or improve his or her effort.

FINDINGS: Kraft and Dougherty found that on average, students in the control group became less engaged over time: Their homework completion rate decreased by more than 6.5 percentage. Students in the treatment group maintained their initial levels of engagement and improved their behavior: Their homework completion rate only dropped by 0.6 percentage points. Across all measures, teacher-family communication had a large and positive effect on student engagement.

CONCLUSIONS: This study found large and immediate effects of daily teacher-parent and teacher-student communication on homework completion rates, classroom behavior, and participation in class. These are outcomes that have been found to be key in student academic achievement. Nevertheless, the authors note that the context in which their study and experiment took place is particular: It occurred during the summer, a time when teachers may have more time to make phone calls home to their students' families. Also, they were only able to observe the impact of the communication for a short period of time. They suggest that follow-up studies and experiments take a longitudinal look—to see if constant communication throughout the academic year has similar effects on student engagement. As they note, "Although we do not yet know the parameters of an optimal communication strategy, these findings strongly suggest that formalized and frequent teacher–family communication can have an immediate effect on important mediators of student academic achievement" (p. 220).

CONSIDERATIONS FOR THE FIELD: This study shows a promising blueprint for conducting randomized casual experiments in family engagement. The authors chose a particular outcome (student engagement) and, informed by existing research, developed an experiment that isolated the effects of teacher-family and teacher-student communication.

The Underutilized Potential of Teacher-to-Parent Communication: Evidence From a Field Experiment

Matthew A. Kraft and Todd Rogers • 2015

SUMMARY: While several publications have established the positive association between parent involvement and student success, this article explores the causal mechanisms behind the relationship. The study examines a light-touch communication intervention that sent weekly messages from teachers to parents of high school students attending a summer credit recovery program in a large urban school district in the Northeastern U.S., with aims of "increasing parents' efforts and effectiveness at supporting their child's success in school."

BACKGROUND: This study explores how parent-child interactions can increase student performance with weekly parent-teacher communications as the mechanism. Students and their parents were randomly assigned to one of three conditions: positive information, improvement information, and control. Every family, regardless of treatment, received an introductory phone call in the first week. In the following weeks, those assigned to the positive and improvement treatments received weekly messages by either phone call, email, or text. The research team contracted translators to communicate messages in Spanish, Haitian Creole, Cantonese, and Vietnamese for parents who did not speak English.

FINDINGS: Most students in the control group (84.2 percent) earned the credits for which they were enrolled. Overall, both the weekly messaging interventions decreased the percentage of students who failed to earn course credit from 15.8 percent to 9.3 percent, or a 41 percent reduction. This was primarily the result of decreasing the dropout rate.

CONCLUSIONS: Through its success in improving student attendance and passing rates, this intervention highlights the potential to increase parental involvement in their children's education through policy initiatives. Kraft and Rogers note the significance of designing policies that set specific, achievable expectations for teachers in systems that allow for efficient, effective communication, and their study provides evidence that these conditions are not only possible, but impactful and cost-effective.

CONSIDERATIONS FOR THE FIELD: This study highlights strategies to increase equity by providing a simple, technologically efficient way to communicate with all families regularly, especially by reaching across linguistic divides. The intervention invites emergent bilingual parents into the conversation by translating messages to accommodate the languages of all families, forming a line of communication between school and family, and stimulating conversation at home. In addition, the communication is relatively standardized, requiring little extra time and effort from the teacher to get conversations started.

The Essential Conversation: What Parents and Teachers Can Learn From Each Other

Sara Lawrence-Lightfoot • 2003

SUMMARY: Sara Lawrence-Lightfoot takes a deep look into interactions during parent-teacher conferences. She finds that both parents and teachers are often unprepared, nervous, and anxious during the semi-annual meetings. Lawrence-Lightfoot proposes: (1) The first conference should be a "listening meeting," where teachers learn from parents about their children; (2) Teachers should present stories and anecdotes to give parents insight into their children as students; and (3) The best conferences include the child/student.

BACKGROUND: This book explores the underlying narratives, expectations, and assumptions that shape parent-teacher conferences, and consequently other parent-teacher interactions and relationships. It is based on the experiences and perspectives of ten female teachers and parents of the children in their classrooms and seeks to provide a more detailed and deep understanding of intimate and personal interactions between parents and teachers.

DESIGN OF THE STUDY: Lawrence-Lightfoot uses the method of portraiture to weave together stories and experiences of teachers and parents in schools across the United States. She conducted one-on-one interviews with teachers and parents, and observed conferences. Teachers selected for the study were not only good at their pedagogical practices, but also demonstrated skills, empathy, and care when interacting with parents.

FINDINGS: Findings revealed three "central domains" that impact parent-teacher interactions:

1. **Autobiographical and psychological scripts:** Broader historical and personal narratives influence parent-teacher encounters. Lawrence-Lightfoot calls those narratives "ghosts in the classroom" and they are present without either party knowing. When adults meet in the classroom, their autobiographical experiences unknowingly influence how they relate to one another.

2. **Double-edge nature of conferences:** Parent-teacher conferences can either create a welcoming environment or limit parents and teachers to connect genuinely. The "double-edged nature" is magnified because so much is at stake during the relatively brief interactions.

3. **Variation in relationships:** There is wide variation in parent-teacher interactions depending on matters such as race, class, educational backgrounds, and immigration status. Nevertheless, all parents have educational expectations for their children. Conferences need to address the specific context of families.

CONCLUSIONS: Parent-teacher conferences are embedded with hidden messages, narratives, and unconscious expectations. Lawrence-Lightfoot reveals the dynamics that emerge from them: the "ghosts" that shape how parents and teachers understand each other, the inclination of ritual, and the importance of considering context. Becoming aware of these dynamics, Lawrence-Lightfoot notes, is essential to maximize the potential of parent-teacher conferences, and concludes that teachers need: (1) to be trained in the art of observation; (2) to be trained in record-keeping or journaling; and (3) to learn to listen to parents and be open and receptive to parental insights.

CONSIDERATIONS FOR THE FIELD: Developing authentic relationships and trust with parents begins with open lines of communication. Teachers bear the responsibility of easing tensions and welcoming parents into their classrooms. They can acknowledge their "ghosts" and interrogate them to understand how they may be unconsciously shaping interactions with parents. This reflective work can and should happen in teacher training programs and professional development sessions.

Parents 2018: Going Beyond Good Grades

Learning Heroes, Edge Research • 2018

SUMMARY: This mixed method study conducted by Learning Heroes examined the disconnect between parents' perceptions of their children's academic proficiency and the reality, and provided engagement tools to help parents and teachers communicate effectively.

BACKGROUND: Learning Heroes gathered data on parents' attitudes and perceptions to better understand how best to equip them with the information they need to help their children succeed (p. 4). The organization's 2018 research sought to address this widespread misconception by identifying the drivers behind the disconnect, as well as exploring what information parents need to have a more accurate, holistic view of their children's progress, and how best to communicate it. Closing this disconnect by giving parents the resources they need may help them to better assist their children in attaining goals and aspirations.

DESIGN OF STUDY: Researchers gathered qualitative data from across nationwide contexts in Grades 3–8 through parent focus groups and educator interviews, and conducted two national online surveys of parents and educators of students in Grades 3–8.

FINDINGS: While most parents were generally overconfident in their child's academic performance, they differed in terms of how they engage with education and their openness to new information. Both parents and teachers recognize the importance of parent involvement, but they have different perceptions of what strong involvement looks like and how much of it is happening. This disconnect is present in how teachers and parents evaluate report cards as well—teachers use a variety of data points to measure student performance that are not laid out on a report card itself, leading some parents to interpret a higher grade as academic proficiency. Most teachers agree that communicating with parents to provide a clear picture of their child's performance is important, but barriers such as lack of training or administrative support make this a challenge.

CONCLUSION: This report finds three key insights: that different parenting styles affect how parents engage in their children's education, report cards are a central source of disconnect between parent and teacher concerns and priorities, and that bridging this disconnect is achievable.

CONSIDERATIONS FOR THE FIELD: This report emphasizes the necessity for effective parent-teacher communication and how equitable partnerships with families can engender mutual understanding between teachers, students, and parents. Competing definitions of engagement and proficiency come into play, and school-family partnerships should incorporate interpretations from different spheres of influence in order to build equitable relationships. Bridging the divides between families and school staff is essential to truly shared investment in student success.

Engaging Families to Support Students' Transition to High School: Evidence from the Field

Martha Abele MacIver, Joyce L. Epstein, Steven B. Sheldon, and Ean Fonseca • 2015

SUMMARY: This correlational study found that efforts by middle and high schools to help students and families prepare for the transition from one to the other significantly reduce the proportion of ninth graders who are struggling academically.

BACKGROUND: Ninth grade is a critical year in students' school careers. Adjusting to a more complex school environment is a challenge that vulnerable students need extra support to meet. This study explores how middle and high schools can partner with families to help their students successfully navigate this transition and stay engaged through graduation.

DESIGN OF STUDY: This exploratory study examines how middle grades and high schools engage families as their students made the transition to high school. The authors analyzed variations in schools' implementation of transition activities, including the following:

- Inviting incoming students and parents to visit the school before the start of the year.
- Communicating with parents before the start of the year about the high school's expectations for students' attendance, behavior, and achievement.
- Communicating with parents during the year on how to monitor their child's progress.
- Informing parents about the school's family engagement program, including the ATP.
- Joining with sending school to prepare students and families to move on.
- Communicating with families about how to support their child's transition to high school.

FINDINGS: The most significant finding was that the percentage of students who struggle academically was highly related to the extent and quality of the schools' transition programs and the percentage of parents who were able to guide their children's learning.

CONCLUSIONS: Family engagement in high school is far more than just checking on attendance and homework. It also entails coaching and guiding students to construct their identities as students, set goals for earning the credits to graduate, and plan for their futures. When parents understand the importance of a smooth transition to ninth grade, the courses students must pass to qualify for a post-secondary program, and the requirements for on-time graduation, the better they can encourage and guide their students toward meeting their goals. Districts and schools must take responsibility for building families' capacity to be partners with schools in ensuring all students can have a productive future.

CONSIDERATIONS FOR THE FIELD: This study suggests that helping middle and high schools develop better transition programs for students and families can improve student outcomes in all types of school settings, especially those serving low-income areas. At least part of the persistent achievement gap stemming from income inequality can be explained by disparities in families' understanding of how to help their students navigate high school. It is incumbent upon schools to remedy this disparity. Where else will families get the information, access, and support they need to work as partners with educators?

Mindset Shifts and Parent-Teacher Home Visits

Katherine McKnight, Nitya Venkateswaran, Jennifer Laird, and Jessica Robles • 2017

SUMMARY: The Parent-Teacher Home Visits (PTHV) model is designed to promote a trusting, mutually supportive relationship between educators and families. This qualitative study, based on interviews with 175 teachers and parents, found that PTHV helps to interrupt implicit biases that educators and families may have about each other. These mindset shifts operate to improve partnerships between educators and families and support student success.

BACKGROUND: In this study, the authors examined whether and how the Parent-Teacher Home Visits (PTHV) model helps to interrupt implicit biases. Referred to as "mindset shifts," these changes may enable educators and families to partner more effectively to support student success, especially when they come from a different race, class, or cultural background than their students. In the PTHV model, educators are trained and then invite their students' families to host a home visit. All visits are done by a team of two teachers who discuss hopes and dreams that family members have for their students.

DESIGN OF STUDY: The study relies on three sources of data: 1) research on implicit biases; 2) a field scan of other home visit programs; and 3) qualitative data collected from two or three schools in each of four large districts implementing PTHV. Each district serves a majority of students who are of color and from low-income families. The authors interviewed the principals and did focus groups with educators and families at each school, totaling 175 PTHV participants.

FINDINGS: Families shifted beliefs and actions about educators and schools, realizing that interactions with educators did not have to be negative or uncomfortable. This built families' confidence and comfort in reaching out to educators about students' needs. Educators shifted beliefs and actions related to both families and students, recognizing that many assumptions they held were unfounded. This new understanding and empathy changed educators' behaviors, allowing them to use information obtained from the home visits to improve student engagement and motivation, use less punitive discipline, and communicate effectively with families.

CONCLUSIONS: Counteracting implicit biases is essential to building successful relationships across boundaries of class, race, education, gender, and culture. Creating opportunities for families and educators to meet outside of school, and to get to know each other, breaks down traditional barriers to partnerships. This study suggests that PTHV has strong, research-supported elements for counteracting biases, reducing discriminatory behaviors, and building positive school-family partnerships that center on student success.

CONSIDERATIONS FOR THE FIELD: As the Sheldon and Jung (2018) and Venkateswaran (2018) studies on PTHV show, PTHV is a well-designed model with significant benefits for students, teachers, and families. In particular, the effect of PTHV on implicit bias could prove useful to other programs that are designed to build family-school partnerships. For example, debriefing is a critical component of building self-awareness and motivation to address implicit biases and discriminatory behavior. PTHV should be a core component of a systems approach to decreasing implicit biases and fostering school and family partnerships.

The Way We Do School: The Making of Oakland's Full-Service Community School District

Millbrey McLaughlin, Kendra Fehrer, and Jacob Leos-Urbel • 2020

SUMMARY: This mixed-methods study examined how the Oakland Unified School District developed an enduring system of full-service community schools (FSCS) from 2011–2019. Using the FSCS whole-child model as a system change strategy profoundly altered structure and practice at both district and school levels. Student outcomes have slowly but steadily improved.

BACKGROUND: This book covers the Oakland Unified School District's (OUSD) effort to transform the system, using a whole-child approach as "a way of doing school." Oakland leaders focused on system change to "disrupt inequities" in opportunities available to students and by integrating community resources into the school's academic program. All community schools provide expanded learning opportunities, health and social services, and family/community engagement.

DESIGN OF STUDY: The authors explore whether the FSCS model can produce system change, and if so, how. In the system-level study, McLaughlin's team conducted over 90 interviews with OUSD educators, administrators, community partners, and civic leaders, and analyzed outcome data to create a long-term account of implementation issues and outcomes. In the site-level study, Fehrer and Leos-Urbel interviewed and observed in nine schools, elementary to high school.

FINDINGS: Since 2011, Oakland has created an effective, expanding FSCS initiative, despite five leadership turnovers and budget crises. By 2019, 42 of 86 district schools had a full-time community school manager. By that year, students were visiting 16 school-based health centers; 75 after-school programs attracted 8,000 students a day; and partnerships with 215 community organizations were enriching the school day. All district schools included elements of a FSCS model, such as social-emotional learning strategies and Coordination of Services Teams (COST).

The data show that the FSCS initiative has led to many benefits for students: reduced suspensions and high-risk behaviors, improved school climate and culture, increased family and youth involvement in site-based decisions, and positive student health outcomes. The high school graduation rate increased from 59.3 percent in 2011 to 73.5 percent in 2019.

CONCLUSIONS: This study shows how a community school model can drive change by infusing a "community school mindset" throughout an entire school district. The key is to transform the underlying structures that reinforce the inequities students experience. Taking 18 months to develop a comprehensive plan, in collaboration with families, community members, and local partners, was critical to the success and sustainability of Oakland's FSCS initiative.

CONSIDERATIONS FOR THE FIELD: Community schools offer an "expanded vision of schooling." They see physical and mental health, safety, positive adult connections, expanded learning time, and social supports as integral to children's learning and development. Disparities in resources and opportunities available to young people growing up in concentrated poverty, such as food insecurity, homelessness, and lack of medical care, explain much of the achievement gaps in student outcomes. In short, students can't learn if their basic needs are unmet.

Building Partnerships to Reinvent School Culture: Austin Interfaith

Kavitha Mediratta, Seema Shah, and Sara McAlister • 2009

SUMMARY: This multi-method case study describes how the Austin Interfaith (AI) Alliance Schools parent and community organizing effort yielded new resources for high-poverty, low-performing schools, as well as new skills and relationships among parents, teachers, and administrators. In schools with high-level involvement in the Alliance Schools initiative, students gained from 15 and 19 percentage points on the Texas state assessment, compared to a four percent gain in schools with minimal involvement.

BACKGROUND: Affiliated with the Industrial Areas Foundation (IAF), a national organizing network, AI builds local networks of faith-based institutions and community members to improve local neighborhoods. Aiming to improve low-performing schools in East Austin, AI created a network of "Alliance Schools" in low-income areas. Using community organizing tactics, AI provided leadership training to parents, teachers, and administrators, and developed relationships with the superintendent, school board, and municipal leaders.

DESIGN OF STUDY: The authors focused on how AI influenced schools' capacity to educate students successfully and whether those efforts produced measurable gains in student outcomes. The authors interviewed school and district leaders, local education experts, AI staff and members, and reviewed AI documents and media coverage, responses to teacher surveys, and student outcome data for all schools in the district.

FINDINGS: AI worked with district leaders to create an ESL teacher pipeline program, after-school and summer programs, adult ESL programs, and professional development for teachers and administrators. In schools that were highly involved with AI, teachers rated their school's climate, professional culture, and leadership more highly. Parents reported having greater access to important information, opportunities for communication, and respect from school staff. Students made gains ranging between 15 and 19 percentage points on the state assessment.

CONCLUSIONS: Through the Alliance Schools network, Austin Interfaith engaged in a long-term effort to recruit and train parents and teachers to work together as leaders in a participatory, action-oriented, problem-solving process. Organizers helped to build a collaborative culture in schools that energized the school community with a sense of shared purpose and power.

CONSIDERATIONS FOR THE FIELD: In districts with chronically underperforming schools, a higher level of intervention is required to improve. Working with outside organizers can help create a community with shared purpose. District support and partnerships are essential to sustain the work over the long term. "Reinventing" the culture of failing schools was a useful lens because it allowed the school community to avoid laying blame and share a common purpose.

BUILDING COMMUNITY STARTS WITH LISTENING. To create consensus, teachers and parents embarked on a listening campaign through neighborhood walks and house meetings. The understandings gained transformed the way they saw each other, which altered the way they understood their roles in school improvement and, consequently, how they worked together.

Springboard Summer Reading Program Evaluation Report

Kelly Piccinino, Sarah K. Pepper, Hanna Salomon, Sara Greenfield, and Wendy McClanahan • 2020

SUMMARY: This quasi-experimental study is an external evaluation of Springboard Summer, an intensive, five-week program designed to close gaps in grade-level reading performance by building lasting capacity among students, parents, and teachers. On average, participants across all grades improved their reading scores from the end of the school year by the beginning of the next school year.

BACKGROUND: The Springboard Collaborative approach to reducing literacy gaps aims to close the gap between home and school. Programming provides intensive coaching for both teachers and families to help their primary school students cultivate successful reading habits. Springboard Summer is a five-week summer program that works to reverse summer slide/learning loss in rising kindergarten through fourth grade students.

DESIGN OF STUDY: The study sought to determine how participation in Springboard Summer is associated with reading growth and how participants' reading achievement compares to that of non-participants. 673 Springboard Summer scholars in Grades TK–4 from five districts from across the country were included in the study. Programs took place in either 2018 or 2019.

FINDINGS: On average, scholars across all grades showed improvement in reading assessment scores after completing Springboard Summer. In some instances, all scholars showed significant improvement, while in others, only those starting behind grade level showed it. Generally, though, scholars who started below grade level showed the largest gains. On average and across all grades, Springboard Summer scholars showed significant improvements between end-of-year and beginning-of-year outcomes as compared to matched comparison students.

CONCLUSIONS: Springboard Summer produces marked improvements in literacy for elementary students, especially those that are behind grade level. This is bolstered by a strong focus on family engagement, which engages caretakers as fellow educators essential to their children's academic success.

CONSIDERATIONS FOR THE FIELD: Springboard Summer approaches bridging gaps in literacy with an all-hands-on-deck attitude—intensive capacity-building for not just students, but families and teachers as well. This model uses families as an essential component of academic success.

"Contra la corriente (Against the Current)": The Role of Latino Fathers in Family-School Engagement

Sandra Quiñones & Judy Marquez Kiyama • 2014

SUMMARY: This study examined the role and perspectives of Latino fathers in family-school engagement. Focusing on the experiences of eight Puerto Rican fathers with children in a low-performing urban school district in New York State, the study looked at how Latino fathers' engagement in their children's education could be understood as moving *contra la corriente*, or going against the current: they reported constantly navigating people and systems that seemed to push back. Yet, they refused to give up and the findings reveal that school systems need to collaborate with them to ensure educational equity.

BACKGROUND: To improve the educational outcomes of Latino students, Quiñones and Kiyama specifically focused on the role and perceptions of Latino fathers regarding family-school relationships. Existing research has rarely focused on Latino fathers and the authors point to them as important "untapped resource" to positively impact educational outcomes.

FINDINGS: During the focus groups, the Latino fathers shared their educational aspirations for their children: They wanted their children to have access to a good education and to have a prosperous future. They engaged in what Quiñones and Kiyama call "dominant middle-class approaches to parental involvement," such as monitoring their children's grades, assisting them with homework when possible, and attending in-school events. All the participants believed that a good education, a *buena educación*, begins in the home and extends to the schools, highlighting the importance of home-school-community relationships. Quiñones and Kiyama note that Latino fathers take the roles of cultivators, critics, defenders, and advocates in their children's education.

CONCLUSIONS: The study's findings illustrate how Latino fathers are engaged in their children's education and how they perceive their roles. As the authors note, the fathers did not always trust schools to have their children's or the broader Latino community's best interests at heart. The fathers believed they had to be extra vigilant and critical of school and district personnel to counter the invisibility they perceived. As the authors note, the fathers "were intentionally playing 'the game' not just because someone told them they should be involved, but because they understood that in order to progress, they had to play by the rules of the middle class, while at the same time critiquing in and their place in it."

CONSIDERATIONS FOR THE FIELD: This study not only showed how many Latino fathers are engaged in their children's education, even if they have to fight *contra la corriente*, but also the different roles they take on: cultivators, critics, defenders, and advocates. To further support the educational outcomes of Latina/o students, it is important for schools and communities to intentionally partner with fathers. Understanding these different roles serves as a necessary first step to accomplish this.

The Development and Sustainability of School-Based Parent Networks in Low-Income Latinx Communities: A Mixed Methods Investigation

David Rangel, Megan N. Shoji, and Adam Gamoran • 2020

SUMMARY: Interviews and survey data with 3,000 low-income, Latinx families reveal how the size and quality of parent networks change over time in the presence of Families and Schools Together (FAST), a family engagement program. This study identifies the factors that lead to building high-quality networks of mutual support: trust, expressing care and respect, and reciprocity.

BACKGROUND: Although schools play a central role in connecting families, there appears to be a disconnect between schools and low-income Latinx families. This study addresses two questions: How do parents meet other parents—and does a program designed to facilitate their connections make a difference? What conditions nourish more trusting relationships among parents?

DESIGN OF STUDY: To investigate how parents describe meeting other parents in the elementary school community, the authors used in-depth structured interviews and quantitative survey data. In the parent interviews, the authors asked about what conditions they feel are critical for trusting relationships to develop. The data came from a randomized controlled trial of FAST, an after-school program that engages families in group activities.

FINDINGS: When people say they "know" another person, they still might not be "friends." Friends have trusting relationships and provide each other material, social, or emotional support.

In a typical school, parents meet others as they pick up and drop off their children at school. Schools are rarely mentioned as connectors to other families. FAST increased the quality of relationships among parents from first through third grade. Once parents no longer took part in the FAST program, however, the ratings of quality relationships reverted to about the same as the comparison schools. This suggests that few schools provide opportunities for parents to meet and interact in ways that yield supportive networks.

CONCLUSIONS: The struggle that urban schools face to engage parents may stem from relying on traditional forms of engagement, such as parent-teacher organizations and school volunteer programs. Such efforts fail to address structural obstacles, such as language barriers, trouble navigating complex institutions, and economic constraints. To build families' social capital by developing networks of close friendships requires a level of connection that allows parents to determine trustworthiness, express care and respect for one another, and exchange favors. Most common events at school are not designed to do this, and parents report they rarely talk to others at such events.

CONSIDERATIONS FOR THE FIELD: The authors exhort schools to provide frequent opportunities for parents to meet and interact throughout the year, including facilitated get-to-know-you activities. Schools can also open a parent room with books and toys to borrow, informational materials, and informal discussion groups where families can gather when they come to school.

Parental Involvement and Children's School Success

Arthur Reynolds and Melissa Clements • 2005

SUMMARY: This long-term, quantitative study of the Chicago Parent Centers documents a significant, even dramatic, relationship between parent engagement and positive social and academic outcomes for children. Children whose parents took part in the program had a 21 percent higher graduation rate than children who did not have that advantage.

BACKGROUND: Chicago Parent Centers (CPC) is a center-based, early intervention program that provides education and family support services to low-income children and parents from ages 3–9. The theory of change is that children's readiness for school can be enriched through family support and language-learning activities. Direct parent involvement in CPC is designed to enhance parent-child interactions, parent and child attachment to school, social support among parents, and children's school readiness and social adjustment.

DESIGN OF STUDY: The Chicago Longitudinal Study data base for this study consists of 1,539 low-income children—93 percent African American—who took part in Chicago Child-Parent Center program (beginning in 1983–84) and a matched comparison group enrolled in an alternative kindergarten intervention. The study continued for 17 years.

FINDINGS: CPC participation at ages three or four is associated with educational and social outcomes that continue up to 18 years after the end of intervention. The longer parents took part in the program, and the more they were involved at school, the more likely their children were to complete high school, and the less likely they were to repeat a grade, be arrested, or require special education. Participation in the CPC program contributed to children's motivation, cognitive ability, social adjustment, family support, and school support.

The researchers estimate that the cost-benefit of the CPC program would save seven dollars for every dollar invested in the preschool component, through reductions in remedial education and criminal justice costs. About $2 out of the $7 can be attributed to the family support program. Every year that a parent remains involved in their child's learning (as rated by teachers) brings a 16 percent increase in the odds of high school completion.

CONCLUSIONS: Reynolds and Clements find that programs that provide child education and intensive resources for parent engagement yield greater and longer-lasting benefits than many efforts that consume a larger share of public spending (e.g., small class size, after-school programs, and dropout prevention). It is important, however, that early education programs be high quality: they should span at least the first five years of life, include well-trained preschool teachers and content to promote children's literacy learning, and feature intensive family involvement activities.

CONSIDERATIONS FOR THE FIELD: The striking results of this study have deep implications for how districts and schools use their federal Title I funds, at least one percent of which must be used to engage families. The Chicago Parent-Child Centers program is funded largely from this source. It is important to ask how a school district is using its Title I money, and what impact on children's learning and development is the current strategy having.

Principal Leadership for School, Family, and Community Partnerships: The Role of a Systems Approach to Reform Implementation

Mavis G. Sanders • 2014

SUMMARY: This article depicts how two school districts (one urban, one suburban) engaged in a systems approach to family-school-community engagement reform developed by the National Network of Partnership Schools (NNPS). The author describes how district-level expectations, policies, and practices affected principals' leadership and action around family and community engagement.

BACKGROUND: To understand how district leaders implemented and scaled the NNPS approach to family-school-community partnerships, Sanders designed a five-year qualitative study in four districts across the United States. The focus of this article are District 3, an urban district, and District 4, a suburban district. Data collection included a phenomenological, semi-structured focus group and informal interviews; observations of workshops, meetings, presentations, and other work-related activities of district-level participants; district and NNPS document collection and review; and site visits to schools participating in the NNPS programming.

FINDINGS: Sanders found that superintendents and school board members in District 3 and District 4 supported systemwide implementation of the NNPS reform in multiple ways, including attending NNPS district events and activities, using NNPS language and principles in districtwide communications and policies, and allocating funding for NNPS coordinators. Principals who embraced the NNPS reform did so to improve their schools around school climate, student grades, and student attendance. Sanders notes that this buy-in did not occur overnight. Instead, they were facilitated by district coordinators, with the support of superintendents and school board members, and their in-depth professional development sessions where they informed principals about the different elements of the NNPS reform. Buy-in was also sustained by publicly celebrating efforts and achievements.

CONCLUSIONS: This study underlines the importance of a systems-level approach to educational reform: The investment of district leadership in the work of the NNPS led to improved family-school-community partnerships. Additionally, the essential role of NNPS coordinators in this reform highlights the importance of having individuals at the district level focus on partnership work. Their work modeling collaborations with families and community members, doing professional development sessions, and holding principals accountable to school goals led to positive outcomes. This is how, according to Sanders, external reforms can be established and scaled up. Regarding the role of principals, within a systems approach, principal resistance can be reduced and buy-in increased by establishing systems of support and setting accountability measures.

CONSIDERATIONS FOR THE FIELD: This study illustrates the importance of district-level leadership in the implementation of school reforms: it shows that when school-family-community is valued and invested in at the district level, positive outcomes emerge.

Student Outcomes and Parent-Teacher Home Visits

Steven B. Sheldon and Sol Bee Jung • 2018

SUMMARY: This report is the final in a three-study national evaluation of the Parent-Teacher Home Visits (PTHV) model. Schools that systematically implemented PTHV saw decreased rates of student chronic absence and increased rates of ELA and math proficiency. Students whose families were visited were less likely to be chronically absent and to reach proficiency on ELA tests, compared to students whose families did not receive visits. Findings support the implementation of PTHV as an evidence-based family engagement approach to student outcomes.

BACKGROUND: At the center of the PTHV model is the essential role of family-school partnerships. The model focuses on developing and nurturing these relationships and partnerships by building trust and communication and collaborating for student success. PTHV is implemented in over 700 communities in 25 states. Each of these locations develops its own context-specific collaboration between local partners and school districts, community organizations, and teachers' unions. This study focuses on student chronic absenteeism and proficiency in reading and math.

DESIGN OF STUDY: This study focuses on four large, highly diverse districts across the United States. One district is in the Mountain region, one in the Mid-Atlantic region, and two in the West. Researchers had access to data for over 100,000 students in kindergarten through eighth grade, attending hundreds of schools. The first analysis compared outcomes of schools that conducted home visits with at least 10 percent of students' families to those of schools that conducted fewer or no home visits with families. The second focused on the relationship between individual student outcomes and home visits.

FINDINGS: Sheldon and Jung found that the implementation of the PTHV model can support positive outcomes for students and improved rates of attendance and learning at schools. School-level outcomes included decreased chronic absence, improved ELA performance, and improved math performance.

CONCLUSIONS: This study, along with the two previous studies evaluating PTHV, support existing research that suggests that family engagement supports student success. Specifically, these studies support the implementation of the PTHV model which focuses on the development of relationships, trust, and open communication between schools and students' families. Put differently, these studies support the implementation of the PTHV model as an evidence-based family engagement approach to improve student outcomes.

CONSIDERATIONS FOR THE FIELD: This study further illustrates the potential of home visits. A key element to remember about the PTHV model is the importance of fidelity to the five core elements—these set the foundation of the development of relational trust between educators and families. Future studies should consider evaluating other student outcomes.

Family Engagement and Its Impact During Distance Learning: Follow-up Report

TalkingPoints • 2021

SUMMARY: TalkingPoints, a multilingual platform that helps parents and educators communicate, conducted a survey in June 2021 to gauge how family-teacher communication impacted the learning experience after a year of distance learning.

BACKGROUND: TalkingPoints' mission centers around advancing effective family-school partnerships by facilitating meaningful relationship- and capacity-building between parents and teachers. It is a two-way messaging and personalized content platform that helps parents and teachers communicate in more than 100 languages.

STUDY DESIGN: TalkingPoints conducted a survey in June 2021 of 940 families and 497 teachers, all of whom were users of the TalkingPoints platform and generally reflected the nonprofit's clientele demographic. English-, Spanish-, and Portuguese-speaking families were surveyed for their perspectives on communication, family engagement, and the value and impact of family-teacher relationships over the recent period of distance or hybrid learning.

FINDINGS: Survey results yielded four key findings: 1) Both teachers and families view family-teacher communication as a top priority; 2) Frequent communication helps student learning and well-being, especially for students from non-English-speaking families; 3) Conversations that built a deeper understanding of family needs and circumstances increased student success; and 4) There are disconnects and areas for improvement in communication between teachers and families.

CONCLUSION: Through TalkingPoints' multilingual platform, teachers and families were able to strengthen communication and build relationships during the pandemic. Educators increasingly see the value of family-school partnerships in supporting student learning, particularly for families who do not speak English at home, and the distance learning conditions highlighted how this engagement led to improvements in student learning and holistic development. Increasing equity and understanding through accessible, empowering communication across language barriers is key to student success.

CONSIDERATIONS FOR THE FIELD: This report captures the experiences of teachers and parents on either side of these relationships during the COVID-19 pandemic and how they leveraged their learnings for more collaborative and supportive relationships in the future. Connections could be built remotely, and two-way lines of communication were more important than ever before as students returned to the classroom after more than a year of alienation and trauma. Remote learning was able to bridge the gap between home and school through teacher-family communication. Moving in the direction of post-pandemic education, the key will be to maintain and strengthen school-family relationships for more equitable and effective schooling environments.

The Impact of Family Involvement on the Education of Children Ages 3 to 8: A Focus on Literacy and Math Achievement Outcomes and Social-Emotional Skills

Francis L. Van Voorhis, Michelle F. Maier, Joyce L. Epstein, and Chrishana M. Lloyd • 2013

SUMMARY: This literature review summarizes 95 research studies conducted between 2000–2012 "on how families' involvement in children's learning and development through activities at home and at school affects the literacy, mathematics, and social-emotional skills of children ages 3 to 8" (p. iii).

BACKGROUND: While the positive link between family involvement and student outcomes is well-established, it is still unclear how exactly family influence at home affects children's learning, as well as how the establishment of family-school partnerships can lead to positive outcomes. This report reviews the existing research on how family involvement activities at both home and school, including family-school partnerships, affect young children's literacy, math, and social-emotional skills.

DESIGN OF STUDY: Comprising the sample are 95 studies published in peer-reviewed journals between 2000 and 2012 with samples of more than 30 subjects. These include nonexperimental, experimental, and quasi-experimental studies that examined aspects of family involvement in literacy, math, and social-emotional development for children ages 3–8.

FINDINGS: Overall, studies indicate that family involvement positively trends with literacy and math skills in preschool, kindergarten, and early elementary grades. Future research is needed to better understand the impact of family involvement on young children's literacy and math skills, as well as their readiness for school. Parents engaging with their children in a variety of reading and math activities trended with improved outcomes in each subject. Parents from all backgrounds across the studies showed that, with guidance, they were "interested in and able to conduct learning activities at home with their young children" (p. ES-3). In order to guide parents in how to best support their children's learning, schools and stakeholders must actively engage all families, and make this inclusion part of schools' or programs' guiding philosophies.

CONCLUSION: The collection of studies in this review conclude that parent involvement is possible and beneficial across all family backgrounds, and they highlight which areas could be improved and better understood through further research, as well as how this research should inform practice.

CONSIDERATIONS FOR THE FIELD: This meta-analysis establishes that across studies, intervention efforts to engage parents from all backgrounds can be effective when providing them guidance and direction on how to support their children's learning. Schools should focus on equitably engaging all families in order to achieve early childhood development outcomes across the board, which may work to shrink and eliminate achievement gaps.

Parent-Teacher Home Visits Implementation Study

Nitya Venkateswaran, Jennifer Laird, Jessica Robles, and Jennifer Jeffries • 2018

SUMMARY: This qualitative study, done in four large urban school districts, explored the effectiveness of five core practices that define the Parent-Teacher Home Visits model. Most educators, administrators, and family members agreed that all five practices were key to creating positive, collaborative relationships between families and educators. The report also includes useful implementation tips for each practice, which could be broadly applied in the family engagement field.

BACKGROUND: The Parent-Teacher Home Visits (PTHV) program is spreading rapidly across the United States. The second in a series of three, this study examines the program's effectiveness in building productive relationships between families and educators, and in improving student outcomes as a result. All three studies were done in the same four urban school districts, all serving mostly students of color from low-income families. All participating sites follow five core practices:

- Visits are voluntary for both educators and families.
- Teachers are trained in how to make the visits and compensated for their time.
- The focus of the first visit is relationship-building, not solving academic or behavior issues.
- Students are not targeted. All students, or a cross-section, receive a visit.
- Educators conduct visits in pairs and reflect afterwards with their partners.

DESIGN OF STUDY: The authors collected data from two main sources: (1) interviews from three or four schools in each of four large districts implementing PTHV, and (2) video observations of a PTHV training from each district. Participating in interviews were a total of 187 people: 105 teachers and staff members, 59 adult family members, 13 school administrators, 8 central office administrators, and 2 PTHV founders.

FINDINGS: Most educators, administrators, and family members agreed that the five core practices ensured that home visits resulted in positive relationships between educators and families. The interviews and observations yielded useful information about how to implement PTHV, from the district level to individual schools.

CONCLUSIONS: The interviews with teachers, family members, and administrators affirm the importance of the model's five core practices. As a result, the authors conclude that these practices should remain "non-negotiables" of the model. Not only are these practices central to the PTHV design, but they also are essential to its successful implementation.

CONSIDERATIONS FOR THE FIELD: The trust that emerges from deep and respectful conversation between families and teachers is the soil in which other efforts to improve student learning can take root. These studies on PTHV strongly suggest that taking the time to have one-on-one, relationship-building conversations centered on the shared goal of student success is well worth the investment.

A Match on Dry Grass: Community Organizing as a Catalyst for School Reform

Mark R. Warren and Karen L. Mapp • 2011

SUMMARY: This multi-case qualitative study provides an understanding of the methods, processes, and capacities through which community organizing works to create and support equity- and justice-oriented school reform. The study reveals how organizing groups build the participation and leadership of parents and students to become powerful actors in school improvement efforts and how community organizing builds powerful relationships that lead to the transformational change necessary to advance educational equity and a robust democracy.

BACKGROUND: The study was designed to build on and add to existing research by identifying and examining the key processes through which organizing groups worked to bring parents, young people, community residents, and educators together to build the capacity for change. The purpose of the study was to dig deeply into the "how" of organizing and gain a deeper understanding of the definition, traditions, processes, and strategies of education organizing.

DESIGN OF STUDY: The study was undertaken as a collaborative qualitative effort among faculty members and graduate students at the Harvard Graduate School of Education. Student researchers formed six case teams and shaped a research process authentic to each locality. On average, each team conducted about 50 formal, one-hour, in-depth interviews with participants at the research sites. Teams also spoke informally with individuals and conducted a small number of focus groups. Teams analyzed their data and wrote the case chapters for the book.

FINDINGS: The book offers a framework to help understand different forms of community organizing. The researchers chose the metaphor of a tree to represent aspects of community organizing, for example, that organizing is a phenomenon that grows and develops and that organizing efforts take time to mature through intentional cultivation and nurturing.

The study found that strong forms of organizing achieve transformation at three levels: the individual, the community, and at the institutional level.

CONCLUSIONS: The study argues that community organizing offers a powerful alternative to the top-down, expert-driven approach typical of many educational reform efforts. Contrary to some views of community organizing efforts, organizing begins with conversation at the ground level, and builds broad participation among parents, young people, and community residents, as well as teachers and educators who often feel voiceless during reform initiatives. Through the process of organizing, all members of a school community have an opportunity to have "ownership of the process of change," resulting in change efforts that are deep and lasting.

CONSIDERATIONS FOR THE FIELD: Organizing provides the "how" of connecting reform to the process of achieving social justice. This analysis of the six community organizing groups in this study offers important lessons and strategy examples for those serious about co-design, inclusivity, and how to engage and include families, young people, and community members in the process of educational reform meaningfully and equitably.

From Private Citizens to Public Actors: The Development of Parent Leaders Through Community Organizing

Mark R. Warren, Karen L. Mapp, and Paul Kuttner • 2015

SUMMARY: This qualitative study explores how community organizing strategies can help individual parents activate their capacities to be leaders in schools and communities. Through the stories of two parent leaders, the authors identify six key processes through which parents emerged as public leaders and advocates in their school communities.

BACKGROUND: A growing body of research looks to community organizing strategies as ways to meaningfully engage families in education, as these groups focus on helping people build the capacity to work together and make change for themselves. This emphasis on building social capital and fostering leadership development with parents is particularly effective in communities that face structural racial and class inequalities that limit engagement with their public schools.

DESIGN OF STUDY: Data is drawn from research conducted as part of a multicase study on community organizing and school reform that culminated in Warren and Mapp's *A Match on Dry Grass* (see Warren et al., 2011). "From Private Citizens to Public Actors" explores the experiences and reflections of two parents in the Northwest Bronx Community and Clergy Coalition. Analysis is supplemented by quotes from other parents who participated in the larger study.

FINDINGS: Organizing groups enabled parents to undergo transformational change from private citizens to public actors and change agents through six processes: listening, building parent community, mentoring, encouraging risk-taking, learning through action, and linking the personal and political.

CONCLUSIONS: This study highlights the importance of engaging families on a personal, collaborative level in order to work toward educational equity. The study illustrates how the problems in public schools are rooted in structural inequalities that need to be addressed by organizing from the ground up. Community organizing strategies that offer parents avenues to personal transformation and solidarity-building lay the groundwork for educational improvement through shared collective power.

CONSIDERATIONS FOR THE FIELD: The insights laid out here provide a road map to scaffolding transformational change in parents by centering their voices and experiences. Their stories provide lived examples of how community organizing strategies can activate the capacities of the actors necessary to organic change in both schools and the community at large.

Evaluation of the FASTalk Program in Oakland Unified School District

Keith Welch • 2018

SUMMARY: This quasi-experimental study evaluated the impact of FASTalk, a school-home text-messaging program designed to improve English Language learning. During the 2017–2018 school year, teachers in 11 mostly Latinx kindergarten and transition-K classes in Oakland, California, sent parents text messages three times a week with tips and activities. After seven months, FASTalk students made between 0.5 and 1.1 months of additional growth compared to students in a matched group whose families did not participate. Students whose home language was different from their teacher's made even greater gains. Finally, students whose families participated more fully, sending at least five messages back to teachers, did better than FASTalk students whose families responded less often.

BACKGROUND: The FASTalk program in Oakland Unified School District (OUSD) used text messages to help families learn strategies to support literacy development in their Pre-K and Kindergarten children. At the beginning of the 2017–18 school year, Family Engagement Lab trained 41 OUSD Transitional Kindergarten and Kindergarten teachers. Each teacher personally signed up families to participate in the program. FASTalk then developed three text messages per week that teachers sent to enrolled parents. These messages contained developmentally appropriate literacy information and activities for parents to engage with their child. All messages were translated into the family's home language.

DESIGN OF STUDY: This evaluation used a quasi-experimental research design called "propensity score matching" to estimate the effect of the FASTalk program on the students' early literacy development. The evaluation examined the effect of the program on student growth using an index of early literacy–related standards-based report card scores over seven months, from November 2017 to June 2018.

FINDINGS: The estimated effect of FASTalk was between 0.5 and 1.1 months of additional growth. Students whose home language differed from their teacher's language grew by an estimated 1.64 to 2.78 more months on the literacy report card index. Students whose parents sent at least five messages to the FASTalk program grew by an estimated 1.94 to 2.14 more months on the literacy report card index than a matched comparison group whose parents sent fewer messages.

CONCLUSIONS: FASTalk appears to be as effective with ELL students as with English-speaking students. Not only did students in the program make gains significantly greater than matched comparison group students, but also those students whose parents participate more frequently made even greater gains.

CONSIDERATIONS FOR THE FIELD: Text-messaging communications programs can build parent-teacher collaboration to foster young children's literacy skills, if they are aligned with the school's literacy program and foster two-way exchange. Teachers can implement these programs easily and with little effort.

REFERENCES

Allensworth, E., Ponisciak, S., & Mazzeo C. (2009). The schools teachers leave: Teacher mobility in Chicago public schools. *Consortium on Chicago School Research*. https://consortium.uchicago.edu/sites/default/files/2018-10/CCSR_Teacher_Mobility.pdf

Angrist, N., Bergman, P., Brewster, C., & Matsheng, M. (2020). Stemming learning loss during the pandemic: A rapid randomized trial of a low-tech interventions in Botswana. *AEA Randomized Controlled Trials*. https://doi.org/10.1257/rct.6044

Ascher, C., & Maguire, C. (2007). Beating the odds: How thirteen NYC schools bring low-performing ninth graders to timely graduation and college enrollment. Annenberg Institute for School Reform at Brown University. https://www.annenberginstitute.org/sites/default/files/BTO_Report.pdf

Baker, T. L., Wise, J., Kelley, G., & Skiba, R. J. (2016) Identifying barriers: Creating solutions to improve family engagement. *School Community Journal, 26*(2), 161–184. https://files.eric.ed.gov/fulltext/EJ1124003.pdf

Barbour, L., Eisenstadt, N., Goodall, J., Jelley, F., & Sylva, K. (2018). Parental engagement fund study. The Sutton Trust. https://www.suttontrust.com/wp-content/uploads/2020/01/Parental-Engagement-Fund-Final-Report.pdf

Baxter, G., & Toe, D. (2021). Teachers use of social media for family engagement, *Educational Action Research*. https://doi.org/10.1080/09650792.2021.1930087

Bryk, A. S., & Schneider, B. (2002). *Trust in schools: A core resource for improvement*. Russell Sage Foundation.

Bryk, A. S., Sebring, P. B., Allensworth, E., Luppescu, S., & Easton, J. Q. (2010). *Organizing schools for improvement*. University of Chicago Press.

Caspe, M., & Lopez, M. E. (2018). Preparing the next generation of librarians for family and community engagement. *Journal of Education for Library and Information Science, 59*(4), 157–178. http://doi.org/10.3138/jelis.59.4.2018-0021

Coleman, J. S. (1966). *Equality of educational opportunity*. U.S. Dept. of Health, Education, and Welfare, Office of Education.

Connecticut State Department of Education. (2018, August). *Full, equal and equitable partnerships with families*. CT.gov. https://portal.ct.gov/SDE/Publications/Full-Equal-and-Equitable-Partnerships-with-Families

Cuevas, S. (2019). "Con mucho sacrificio, we give them everything we can": The strategic sacrifices of undocumented Latina/o parents. *Harvard Educational Review, 89*. 473–496. https://doi.org/10.17763/1943-5045-89.3.473.

Flores, O. J., & Kyere, E. (2020). Advancing equity-based school leadership: The importance of family–school relationships. *Urban Review, 53*(1), 127–144. https://doi.org/10.1007/s11256-020-00557-z

Geller, J., Luiz, J., Asher, D., McAlister, S., Henderson, A. T., Kressley, K. G., Perez, W., & Sanzone, J. eds. (2019). The ripple effect in action: What seven parent leadership initiatives learned from participatory evaluation. *NYU Metropolitan Center for Research on Equity and the Transformation of Schools*. https://parentleadershipevaluation.steinhardt.nyu.edu/sites/default/files/inline-files/PLEN_Synopsis_FINAL.pdf

Ginwright, S. (2016). *Hope and healing in urban education: How urban activists and teachers are reclaiming matters of the heart*. Routledge.

Hammond, L. A., & Ferlazzo, L. (2009). *Building parent engagement in schools*. ABC-CLIO, Linworth Publishing Company.

Harris, A. (2020). Evaluation of the FASTalk program: Findings brief. *Family Engagement Lab*. http://www.familyengagementlab.org/uploads/1/0/0/1/100109266/rsl_impact_overview___technical_appendix.pdf

Hayakawa, M., Englund, M. M., Warner-Richter, M. N., & Reynolds, A. J. (2013). The longitudinal process of early parent involvement on student achievement: A path analysis. *NHSA Dialog, 16*(1), 103–126.

Henderson, A. T. (1981). *Parent participation-student achievement: The evidence grows*. National Committee for Citizens in Education.

Henderson, A. T. (1987). *The evidence continues to grow: Parent involvement improves student achievement*. National Committee for Citizens in Education.

Henderson, A. T., & Berla, N. (1994). *A new generation of evidence: The family is critical to student achievement*. National Committee for Citizens in Education.

Henderson, A. T., & Mapp, K. L. (2002). *A new wave of evidence: The impact of school, family, and community connections on student achievement*. National Center for Family & Community Connections with Schools, SEDL.

Henderson, A. T., Mapp, K. L., Johnson, V. R., & Davies, D. (2007). *Beyond the bake sale: The essential guide to family-school partnerships*. The New Press.

Hong, S. (2011). *A cord of three strands: A new approach to parent engagement in schools*. Harvard Education Press.

Hong, S. (2019). *Natural allies: Hope and possibility in teacher-family partnerships*. Harvard Education Press.

Hoover-Dempsey, K. V., Walker, J. M. T., Sandler, H. M., Whetsel, D., Green, C. L., Wilkins, A. S., & Closson, K. E. (2005). Why do parents become involved? Research findings and implications. *Elementary School Journal, 106*(2), 105–130. https://doi.org/10.1086/499194

Humphrey, N., & Squires, G. (2011). Achievement for all national evaluation: Final report. *Department for Education*. https://assets.publishing.service.gov.uk/government/uploads/system/uploads/attachment_data/file/193254/DFE-RR176.pdf

Ishimaru, A. M. (2014). When new relationships meet old narratives: The journey towards improving parent-school relations in a district-community organizing collaboration. *Teachers College Record, 116*(2), 1–56. https://doi.org/10.1177/016146811411600206

Ishimaru, A. M. (2019). From family engagement to equitable collaboration. *Educational Policy, Vol. 33*(2), 350–385. https://doi.org/10.1177/0895904817691841

Ishimaru, A. M. (2020). *Just schools: Building equitable collaborations with families and communities*. Teachers College Press.

Jensen, K. L., & Minke, K. M. (2017). Engaging families at the secondary level: An underused resource for student success. *School Community Journal, 27*(2), 167–191. https://www.adi.org/journal/2017fw/JensenMinkeFall2017.pdf

Kiyama, J. M. (2010). College aspirations and limitations: The role of educational ideologies and funds of knowledge in Mexican American families. *American Educational Research Journal, 47*(2), 330–356. https://doi.org/10.3102/0002831209357468

Kraft, M. A., & Dougherty, S. M. (2013). The effect of teacher–family communication on student engagement: Evidence from a randomized field experiment. *Journal of Research on Educational Effectiveness, 6*(3), 199–222. https://doi.org/10.1080/19345747.2012.743636

Kraft, M. A., & Rogers, T. (2015). The underutilized potential of teacher-to-parent communication: Evidence from a field experiment. *Economics of Education Review, 47*, 46–63. https://scholar.harvard.edu/files/todd_rogers/files/empirical_in_press.kraft_rogers.pdf

Lawrence-Lightfoot, S., & Davis, J. H. (1997). *The art and science of portraiture*. Jossey-Bass.

Lawrence-Lightfoot, S. (2003). *The essential conversation: What parents and teachers can learn from each other*. Ballantine Books.

Learning Heroes, Edge Research. (2018, December). *Parents 2018: Going beyond good grades*. Learning Heroes. https://r50gh2ss1ic2mww8s3uvjvq1-wpengine.netdna-ssl.com/wp-content/uploads/2018/12/2018_Research_Report-final_WEB.pdf

Lowenhaupt, R., & Montgomery, N. (2018). Family engagement practices as sites of possibility: Supporting immigrant families through a district-university partnership. *Theory Into Practice: Imagining Sites of Possibility in Immigrant and Refugee Education, 57*(2), 99–108. https://doi.org/10.1080/00405841.2018.1425814

MacIver, M. A., Epstein, J. L, Sheldon, S. B., & Fonseca, E. (2015). Engaging families to support students' transition to high school: Evidence from the field. *The High School Journal. 99*(1), pp. 27–45. Published by: University of North Carolina Press.

Mapp, K. L. (2012). *Title I and parent involvement lessons from the past: Recommendations for the future*. Center for American Progress. https://www.aei.org/wp-content/uploads/2012/03/-title-i-and-parental-involvement_091556561921.pdf?x91208

Mapp, K. L., & Bergman, E. (2019). *Dual capacity-building framework for family-school partnerships (Version 2)*. www.dualcapacity.org

Mapp, K. L., & Bergman, E. (2021) *Embracing a new normal: Toward a more liberatory approach to family engagement*. https://www.carnegie.org/publications/embracing-new-normal-toward-more-liberatory-approach-family-engagement/

McKnight, K., Venkateswaran, N., Laird, J., & Robles, J (2017). Mindset shifts and parent-teacher home visits. *RTI International*. https://doi.org/10.13140/RG.2.2.27018.36801

McLaughlin, M., Fehrer, K., & Leos-Urbel, J. (2020). *The way we do school: The making of Oakland's full-service community school district*. Harvard Education Press.

Mediratta, K., Shah, S., & McAlister, S. (2009). *Building partnerships to reinvent school culture: Austin interfaith: The case of Texas*. Annenberg Institute for School Reform, Brown University.

Moll, L. C. (2019). Elaborating funds of knowledge: Community-oriented practices in international contexts. *Literacy Research: Theory, Method, and Practice Vol. 68*, 130–138.

Peña, D. C. (2000) Parent involvement: Influencing factors and implications. *The Journal of Educational Research, 94*(1), 42–54. https://doi.org/10.1080/00220670009598741

Piccinino, K., Pepper, S. K., Salomon, H., Greenfield, S., & McClanahan, W. (2020). *Springboard Summer reading program evaluation report*. https://eric.ed.gov/?id=ED615149

Quiñones, S., & Kiyama, J. M. (2014). "Contra la corriente (against the current)": The role of Latino fathers in family–school engagement. *The School Community Journal, 24*(1), 149–176. https://www.adi.org/journal/2014ss/QuinonesKiyamaSpring2014.pdf

Rangel, D., Shoji, M. N., & Gamoran, A. (2020). The development and sustainability of school-based parent networks in low-income Latinx communities: A mixed methods investigation. *AERA Journal, 57*(6), 2451–2484. https://doi.org/10.3102/0002831220916461

Reynolds, A. J., & Clements, M. (2005). Parental involvement and children's school success. In E. Patrikakou & R. P. Weissberg (Eds.), *School-family partnerships for children's success* (pp. 109–130). essay, Teachers College Press.

Sanders, M. G. (2014). Principal leadership for school, family, and community partnerships: The role of a systems approach to reform implementation. *American Journal of Education, 120*(2), 233–255. https://doi.org/10.1086/674374

Sheldon, S. B., & Jung, S. B. (2018). (rep.). *Student outcomes and parent-teacher home visits. Parent Teacher Home Visits and Johns Hopkins University*. https://pthvp.org/wp-content/uploads/2022/03/student-outcomes-and-parent-teacher-home-visits.pdf.

Sheldon, S. (2003). Linking school–family–community partnerships in urban elementary schools to student achievement on state tests. *The Urban Review, 35*(2), 149–165. https://doi.org/10.1023/A:1023713829693

TalkingPoints (2021). *Family engagement and its impact during distance-learning: Follow-up report*. https://talkingpts.org/wp-content/uploads/2021/08/Family-engagement-and-its-impact-during-distance-learning_-follow-up-report.pdf?utm_source=funder-newsletter&utm_medium=textlink&utm_campaign=tl

Tatum, B. D. (2017). *Why are all the black kids sitting together in the cafeteria?: And other conversations about race*. (3rd ed.) Basic Books.

Torre, M. E., & Ayala, J. (2009). Envisioning participatory action research *Entremundos. Feminism & Psychology, 19*(3), 387–393. https://doi.org/10.1177/0959353509105630

Van Voorhis, F. L., Maier, M. F., Epstein, J. L., & Lloyd, C. M. (2013). *The impact of family involvement on the education of children ages 3 to 8: A focus on literacy and math achievement outcomes and social-emotional skills*. MDRC. Retrieved from https://files.eric.ed.gov/fulltext/ED545474.pdf

Venkateswaran, N., Laird, J., Robles, J., & Jeffries, J. (2018). Parent-teacher home visits implementation study (Berkeley CA: RTI International).

Warren, M. R. (2010). *Fire in the heart*. Oxford University Press.

Warren, M. R., & Mapp, K. L. (2011). *A match on dry grass: Community organizing as a catalyst for school reform*. Oxford University Press.

Warren, M. R., Mapp, K. L., & Kuttner, P. (2015). From private citizens to public actors: The development of parent leaders through community organizing. In M.P. Evans & D. B. Hiatt Michael (Eds.), *The power of community engagement for educational change*. Information Age Publishing. 21–39.

Welch, K. (2018). Evaluation of the FASTalk program in Oakland Unified School District: *Family Engagement Lab*. https://www.familyengagementlab.org/uploads/1/0/0/1/100109266/1718_fastalk_eval_findings_brief_.pdf

Williams, D., & Benner, J. (2015). Data inquiry for equitable collaboration: The case of Neighborhood House's data carousel. *The Equitable Parent-School Collaboration Research Project Publication Series*. University of Washington College of Education.

INDEX